KV-579-269

Managing Information – Avoiding Overload

Dr Trevor J Bentley

LIVERPOOL JMU LIBRARY

3   1111   00790   5886

LIVERPOOL
JOHN MOORES UNIVERSITY
AVRIL ROBARTS LRC
TEL. 0151 231 4022

The Chartered Institute of Management Accountants

Copyright © CIMA 1998
First published in 1998 by:
The Chartered Institute of Management Accountants
63 Portland Place
London
W1N 4AB

ISBN 0 7494 2682 9

The publishers of this book consider that it is a worthwhile contribution to discussion, without necessarily sharing the views expressed, which are those of the author.

No responsibility for loss occasioned to any person acting or refraining from action as a result of any material in this publication can be accepted by the author or publishers.

All rights reserved. No part of this publication may be reproduced, stored in a retrieval system, or transmitted, in any form or by any means, electronic, mechanical, photocopying, recorded or otherwise, without the prior permission of the publishers.

Contents

Part III – Information for Decision-making

PART I
The Information Revolution

We are at the present time in the middle of a revolution. Everything seems to be changing and the environment of the workplace is at best turbulent, at worst chaotic. Of course, turbulence and chaos have much to commend them in that the old has to give way to the new, but in the process life is very uncomfortable.

The impact of the information revolution on society, on organisations and on people is highly significant. Old skills have been completely replaced. Young people are growing up in a computer-literate society that has left most of their parents behind. Being informed is now an essential ingredient for success.

Part I of the text covers the impact of the information revolution on society (chapter 1), on organisations (chapter 2) and on individuals (chapter 3). Chapter 4 contains a discussion of the importance of 'getting connected'. Of all the changes that have happened, the development and growth of the Internet has been the most far-reaching, and it has only just started.

1 Social Dimensions of Information

1.1 The wider impact

The information society has arrived. In the Western world more people work with information than in manufacturing or agriculture. Even where work is not directly concerned with information the need to collect and input data imposes demands on workers.

In the workplace, the home, and the high street the impact of information systems is obvious and accepted. There are few places where the demands of the information society can be escaped.

The ideal travelling companion

On a recent train journey, TJ had the dubious pleasure of sitting next to a 'modern business executive' – smartly dressed, with portable phone, portable computer and pocket organiser, all of which were in constant use.

As TJ watched, she took a phone call, referred to her notebook to change a date, and then back to the computer where she typed away, producing a report. Then she made a call, another call came in, then back to the computer.

TJ did not know what she was feeling, but just watching her was making him feel tired. In fact it was interfering with his usual relaxed journey. He tried to concentrate on his book or his crossword, but her phone would ring and she would fly into action. TJ learned a good deal about her business activities, although she probably did not intend him to.

The literacy gap

For young people today computers are part of life. They see nothing unusual in putting their Sky card into its black box to unscramble the television picture. It is unlikely that they think for one moment about the technology involved in the process. Money can be easily obtained from a cash machine, phone calls paid for with a piece of plastic, and the jargon of 'bits' and 'bytes' is like their second language. Young people – those up to 35 years of age, say – are comfortable with and enjoy their contact with computers. They have no fear of the technology and they take all developments in their stride. This age group is highly computer literate.

For older people – at present those up to 55 years old, perhaps – the story is different. They have had to become familiar with computers long after they left school. The jargon is unfamiliar and they have not taken to the information age with the same alacrity as youngsters. There is still resistance to personal use of the technology even when its value is recognised. And it is this age range and older which runs British business. This age group has a poor level of computer literacy.

Generally speaking, any older people have virtually no real understanding of the technology. They don't enjoy their contact with technology. They are uneasy and clumsy with keyboards and mice and have little knowledge of 'icons' or 'windows'. This age group is mostly computer illiterate.

The computer literacy gap has had an interesting impact on working practices and employment. Forty years ago age and experience were highly regarded in most areas of work. Skills develop with experience. Confidence and reliability grow with age and maturity, and this is still true. But today for the over-50s not securely established in work there are few work opportunities. In contrast, young people with technology-based skills are in demand.

For those whose second language is MS-DOS or Java there are many job opportunities. Ageism does not arise because of any underlying prejudice about age, but because the information age is for the young: those over 50 years of age no longer fit. In the information age it is because the young have computer literacy skills that they rule the world.

The world of work

Two hundred and fifty years ago most people worked in, or very near to, their homes. Then, in a period of about 70 years, the way of life of the people and the landscape changed as the industrial revolution took place. People were moved from work on the land or in their own small cottage-based workshops to the new factories. As these factories used steam engines to drive the new large spinning machines they could make more cloth more cheaply, fuelling an explosion in productivity.

Later, this productivity was further extended by the specialisation of labour and the creation of production lines. The economic factors were so powerful that the destruction of village communities and the creation of 'towns of despair' were seen as a way forward to prosperity – at least for the factory owners; the workers were nothing more than slaves. And so today people travel to work in centres of industrial concentration. To match this the administration and control of these massive organisations has been centred in conurbations where large offices have been built. People go to work – the work no longer comes to the people. The exceptions are the artists, artisans, and craftspeople who have managed to retain their independence and home-based activity. In fact, the expression 'home made' is now synonymous with quality, rather than the 'rough and ready' meaning it had 200 years ago. But the wheel is turning full circle.

Working from home

The role of computers and telecoms is a key feature of the return to the cottage industry of the information age.

Homeworkers or teleworkers can provide a cost-effective and productive service in such areas as design, administration, selling, writing, graphics, publishing and editing. The advantages are considerable.

For the individual travelling is reduced, saving time and money and reducing stress. Quality of life is improved. There can also be tax advantages from working at home. For the organisation there is higher staff productivity, lower costs, smaller offices and less absenteeism. There are disadvantages, but these are all to do with an obsolete work ethic which applauds long hours of attendance, regardless of productivity.

Another advantage is a reduction in instances of 'meeting syndrome'. Homeworkers cannot drop what they are doing to 'meet'. Organisations should not see this as a problem, because 90 per cent of meetings are ineffective.

All in all, the move back towards working from home will bring social, personal, and organisational benefits – provided, of course, that it is embraced and not met in the same manner that the Luddites used to try to stop the industrial revolution. Just as they failed, so will those who resist the move away from work as we know it to work as an extension of our daily lives.

Co-operative working

People will increasingly find themselves working in groups using the same data sources via client/server systems. This will happen whether or not people are located at the same site. New groupings and alliances will form and these will move organisations towards project working, where groups from many different parts of the organisation co-operate via the network to carry out specific tasks. This will also impact on the management approaches applicable. People will be paid for what they do rather than for their time, and time boundaries will disappear as markets around the world stay open 24 hours. Accounting systems will have to adapt to different approaches to accountability – possibly on a project or team basis, rather than on a departmental model.

1.2 The economic impact

The information age has brought with it major consequences for both micro- and macroeconomics. If we think of the microeconomic environment of the organisation, and the macroeconomic environment of the marketplace in which the organisation works, we can identify the impact of the information age.

The microeconomics of the organisation

Organisations are groupings of people who gain their economic sustenance from working in the organisation. If the organisation ceases to be economically viable, i.e. if it does not add value and create a surplus, it will not survive. With its demise will follow economic hardship for the employees of the organisation. This is compounded in the information age, when the speed of communications and the speed of market changes demand a highly flexible response. Quality in products and services is now demanded as of right by customers who, being aware of the possibilities of the information age, are not prepared to tolerate delay.

The organisation has to manage its affairs, particularly its information, in a positive and organised fashion so that it can interact quickly with suppliers, customers, and competitors. When marketplaces are worldwide and when organisations function globally across all time zones there is no time for delay in the system. Size is only a partial protection against a fast-moving world. Gaining the competitive edge is perhaps the most important current focus of management attention in every organisation. This means offering customers something extra and desirable in the product or service offered, or offering the same at a lower price, or both. This is achieved in many ways, but the main impact of information is in reducing costs, increasing efficiency and effectiveness, and improving product/service quality.

The macroeconomics of the marketplace

All organisations operate in a global marketplace. Even if the organisation does not import or export directly it will have to compete with those that do. Segmenting markets into geographic and/or demographic areas does not materially help to manage the macroeconomic effects of the information age.

Information has three primary impacts on the macroeconomic agenda:

- market trends;
- research and development; and
- pricing policy.

Market trends are transferred around the world almost instantaneously. Today's best-selling product could be obsolete tomorrow. Information on what is happening in the market in the USA today will affect the market in the UK tomorrow. Of course, the degree of impact will vary from business to business, and from market to market. The speed of information is such that organisations have to function in a constant state of turbulence. Market awareness is the key to being proactive.

Research and development activities move very fast nowadays. Computer design and modelling is used to carry out procedures that might once have taken years of analysis to complete. This means that organisations have to keep constantly up to date with the latest technical and scientific information.

Pricing policy which has traditionally been determined in relation to the local market is increasingly becoming a global issue. The debate about computer game pricing in the UK compared to that in the US has highlighted the need for extending pricing policy beyond the local marketplace. Of course, this does not mean that local markets do not dictate their own pricing needs through patterns of demand, but the focus of pricing policy has to be broadened.

So here we see that if the organisation does not equip itself to obtain information and to influence affairs it will be left at the starting post.

Value-added networks

Value added networks (VANs) are those which are used to add value directly to the organisation's products and services. A direct link between the stores/purchasing system of a company and its suppliers would enable the ordering and delivery procedures to be speeded up and carried out more efficiently, thus adding value to the business. Just-in-time (JIT) systems, which connect production, stores and suppliers via a network, or customer networks, which enable a company to keep a constant flow of information on customer activity to salespeople, would be other examples. Electronic data interchange applications are also value-added networks.

The key in defining a VAN is whether or not the processes and procedures handled by the network actually 'add value' to the company's business operations.

Perhaps the major difference between VANs and other communication networks is that VANs are external networks to which people share and subscribe. For example, ABTA operates a VAN for travel agents to access training courses from their counter-based terminals. Each access to a VAN provides a specific service and is paid for, similar to the idea of pay-TV. VANs also support the work of staff as they need to access information or book, for example, theatre and airline tickets.

The organisation that sets up the VAN is concerned to market it to those wanting access to the information and services it can provide. It is through the subscription charges paid by subscribers that the VAN owners make a financial return. Some VANs may be offered free to members: companies which invite customers and/or suppliers to join a product information and payment system may offer free use of their VAN.

As IT networks spread and the 'information superhighway' develops, more and more services will be offered via VANs, including home banking and armchair shopping.

1.3 Information exchange and markets

Information is money, or money is information. The money markets of the world trade in information. Deals are done and all that happens is that information is changed in the participants' bank accounts. Money is, in fact, invisible.

?

> ### 1.1 Information transfer
>
> Think about your own activities in work and at home and list all the ways that you get things done by simply transferring information from paying bills to booking a theatre ticket. I imagine most of your transactions are done this way.

Information markets

The stock market is another place where information exchange is the primary function. It is now completely computer-based and markets in shares are made on traders' computer screens.

Organisations also exist whose product is information. Reuters is a good example. It sells information on companies, products, markets, etc., and enables organisations to get the information they need without the costs of collecting it for themselves. Other organisations, such as market research companies, exist to gather and analyse information of a particular kind.

Today collecting, analysing, storing, buying and selling information is a business in itself. There is a market in information and this market supports the modern global marketplace.

Paperless trading

Paperless trading is now practical and effective. It requires the exchange of information between suppliers and customers rather than pieces of paper. All the same procedures of ordering, acknowledgement, delivery advice, and invoicing are carried out, but it is all done via computer. When the details are agreed a funds transfer is authorised, again via computer. The savings in time and effort are considerable.

This form of paperless trading is known as electronic data interchange (EDI). It is an expanding method of trading, and as standards are agreed it will expand further. So what are the benefits of EDI?

The benefits fall into three categories:

- competitive advantage
- more efficient operations
- reduced costs.

Competitive advantage comes from being able to react faster and more efficiently to customer needs, including meeting the requirements of just-in-time materials systems. In addition the cost and inconvenience of credit control and sales-ledger management can be reduced.

Efficiency of operations is improved by removing the delays, misunderstandings and errors associated with paper or telephone/voice-based business transactions.

Costs are reduced by eliminating the need for receiving, processing, handling and storing paper. And in addition fewer staff are needed because there is less rekeying of data into computer systems.

1.4 Dependency

Four main problems arise from the dependency that organisations place on their computer systems.

- *The service factor.* If the computer is 'down' no service can be provided. The possibility of not having the computer available seems to have been ignored in developing alternative methods of service provision.
- *The reality factor.* 'I'm sorry sir – you're not on the computer. Are you sure you're a customer?' If the customer is not listed on the computer, perhaps he does not exist! The computer must be right: even in the face of evidence to the contrary the computer triumphs. People are degraded and belittled by this attitude but it persists.
- *The credit factor.* It is far better to have a credit rating than to have cash. The computerised world functions more effectively with the use of plastic cards than with cash. Cash can be withdrawn from machines anywhere in the world – given the correct piece of plastic. But this works only when the computers do.
- *The travel factor.* It is not possible to book a seat on an aeroplane unless the relevant computer is working, even from the ticket desk at the airport. If the computer goes down the plane does not go up, because air traffic control depends on the computer. So, without computers, the possibilities for travel are limited.

1.5 The future

Buying a car

The year is 2015. David has decided to buy a car. He keys in to his multimedia wall screen and selects shopping from the menu.

'What do you want to buy?' the system asks.

'I'm looking for a new car,' David responds.

The system displays a questionnaire on the screen.

When David has completed the questionnaire he presses the 'enter' key and the system responds with a list of the vehicles which meet David's needs. He selects the first on the list and the system presents a video of the vehicle being driven by an expert. When the video is over the system offers David the chance to book a test drive at his convenience. If he does so the local dealers will call for David at his stated time.

David plays through the videos for the cars on his list and then asks for a test drive for two of the cars which appeal to him. The system asks him how he wants to finance his purchase and offers a range of options.

David can process the whole transaction, including funds transfer, via his system.

Future uncertain

The possibilities for information systems in the future are enormous. Three important and far-reaching developments that appear likely to become widespread in the next twenty years are voice recognition, multimedia and funds transfer. The technology exists at the present time, but the systems are not yet in wide use.

- *Voice recognition* will become standard on portable computers, which will become very small without the need for a keyboard, and on PCs and home multimedia sets. The level will be 'limited conversation', which means that the system will converse with a limited vocabulary and in a question/answer mode. The user will be able to question the machine and it will answer and vice versa. There will still be the option of using a keyboard and a mouse and/or a hand-held laser pointer.

  The laser pointer will be the favourite method of selection on home multimedia systems, because of its convenience and the large size of the wall screens.

- *Multimedia* sound–vision computer systems will become as commonplace as the TV is today. They will offer entertainment via satellite and/or cable, education, access to funds-transfer systems, provide home computing, fax and communications, and two-way video transmission – although this might still be an expensive option in 2015. The system will incorporate existing audio, TV, and radio equipment with the facility to incorporate other pieces of equipment as necessary. The compact disk will be the primary medium for feeding the system. Most multimedia screens will be large, flat wall screens with very high resolution. Terrestrial TV and radio will disappear in favour of satellite transmission.

- *Funds transfer* will be widely available by 2015 and the need to visit bank premises will virtually have disappeared. All requirements from overdrafts to mortgages and insurance will be dealt with via a multimedia system. If a face-to-face meeting is required, a specialist will visit the customer in his own home. It is possible that by 2015 banks will still have a few branches to cater for those unable to hook up to a multimedia system, but these will generally provide public multimedia systems with staff to help in their use.

  With truly effective and comprehensive funds transfer, all transactions will take place as soon as deals are finalised, i.e. goods and services delivered. Sales and purchase ledgers will disappear and credit will only exist with the funds supplier.

These ideas should not seem surprising. The only way they might not be realised is through political lobbying or if there are commercial agreements to stop them.

The 21st century will be an exciting one!

1.6 Summary

- Information management will have a significant impact as the computer literacy gap narrows and disappears, and as we change the way we work.
- The traditional economics of the marketplace will have to be reviewed in the light of the speed and extent of information transfer.
- New information markets are opening up and must be exploited to maintain competitive advantage.
- Society is now largely dependent on the information systems and networks which span the globe.
- The future holds significant promise for more extensive use of information infrastructures.

LIVERPOOL JOHN MOORES UNIVERSITY
LEARNING SERVICES

2 Organisational Power and Privacy

This chapter explores the way that organisations are having to adapt to new ways of organising and controlling their activities. The old order of conformity and deference is giving way to a new order of creativity and diversity.

2.1 Limited access

Information is power. Those 'in the know' are able to act more effectively and hence have more power than those who are not.

This power aspect of information is managed in organisations by limiting access to information.

Which colour are you?

An organisation operated a five-colour information dissemination system. It was called the communication control system. Information was printed on coloured paper, the colour depending on the degree to which the information was to be disseminated through the organisation..

- Yellow   General circulation to everybody and for display on notice boards
- Green   Section heads, supervisors and foremen
- Blue   Managers
- Pink   Senior managers
- Red   Executives and directors

Red sheets were further divided into 'secret' and 'top secret'.

The company secretariat maintained circulation lists for each of the colour bands. Promotion to a higher colour band was something to be celebrated, and brought with it the additional power of being party to a higher level of information.

From time to time there were leaks from one level to another and the grapevine was a wonderful way for people to find out what was going on. The system was a very strong force in keeping everybody in their place within the hierarchy. It also caused many problems.

Information access levels

In the modern world of computers a similar approach to the colour system is attained by the use of authority levels and passwords for controlling access to the information held on corporate databases.

The idea behind authority levels is not only to protect the data from misuse, but also to restrict access to information to the chosen few who are deemed to be trustworthy members of the inner management group. It is through the control of access to information that top management retains its power and influence over events – but this is changing.

2.2 Open management

For open management to be effective – i.e. to to be anything other than a management cliché – it has to offer:

- open access to information;
- a structure based on cooperation and teamwork;
- encouragement of diversity and creativity;
- a welcoming atmosphere for change;
- a learning environment.

Open access to information

The basic idea behind open management is that organisational information is accessible by anyone employed by the organisation. The contract of employment used in open management organisations includes an appropriate confidentiality clause. There have to be suitable controls on the databases to record who has accessed data, and there are controls on who can amend and/or delete data records.

Open management cannot exist without open access to information. If access to information is denied then so is the learning, knowledge and capacity to act that flows from having the information. This stultifies and impoverishes the initiative and creativity of the people in the organisation. It also deadens enthusiasm and commitment.

Open access to information does not mean that individuals get the information they need, it means that they can get the information they *think* they need. This increases individual freedom and encourages creativity.

This open access and freedom to look at information is particularly important when performance management and performance-related pay are involved. People have to be able to look at all figures on performance, for *all* business units, not just their own. It should also be possible to see what every individual in the organisation is being paid, including salary and bonuses.

There may be specific situations where sensitive information is withheld from general availability – for example, if the organisation is contemplating the takeover of another business, or is negotiating major contracts. But even in such situations staff should have access to the information as soon as possible.

A structure based on co-operation and teamwork

Hierarchical organisation structures are no longer practical or adaptable enough to cope with the modern speed of change. People need to be able to work together in teams, share information and agree action.

It is likely that these teams will control the different processes of the business rather than be split into artificial functional or geographical groupings. An example of a business process team might be the 'customer satisfaction team'. This group would be responsible for everything from receipt of an enquiry from a customer to after-sales service. This covers the traditional functional groupings of sales, sales-order processing, distribution, warranties, servicing and complaints. Instead of being responsible for an individual part of the process, the team is responsible for the whole process for a group of customers. To achieve this objective, there has to be close cooperation between those involved. A customer services manager would have team members who sell, process orders, distribute or co-ordinate distribution, deal with warranty claims, co-ordinate servicing, and so on. The customer will have the name of a personal contact.

Information systems make this new approach possible by giving all team staff access to the information they need about product availability, customers, deliveries, etc. Each member of the team takes on particular responsibilities and would swap around to learn and develop multiple skills.

Other activities of the business, such as opening a new factory, would be handled by a 'new factory project team' which would be seconded for the duration of the project or contracted from external specialist staff such as architects. Such a project team would take all the decisions associated with the project and its objective would be, for example, to open a new factory on x date, to produce y within a budget of £z.

On completion of the project the team would be relocated to other work with a new project team or a business process team.

Encouragement of diversity and creativity

Every human being is unique, although an individual may display similarities with others. Recognising and encouraging people to exploit their own diversity is a fundamentally different approach from the traditional organisational approach of deference to the existing order.

As more and more of the details (the figures) of business activities become built into information systems there is great opportunity for releasing and using individual diversity. Diversity of age, gender, race, attitudes, interests and abilities all contribute to the richness of the working environment, and the services the team can offer.

Diversity is also closely linked with creativity. If everyone did things in the same way nothing would change. Just as deference requires and enforces conformity, so diversity empowers creativity. Information systems, by removing much of the routine and mundane from our daily work, open the gates to the inherent diversity and creativity of those in the organisation. As one company's products and services become increasingly indistinguishable from another's it is only the people who can make the competitive difference.

If diversity and creativity is constrained, competitive edge is lost.

A welcoming atmosphere for change

Information systems have always been associated with change, and with the kind of change that has generated much resistance. Resistance has often arisen through ignorance rather than any real threat to jobs, but management must still carry the responsibility for it because it was management that had failed to inform the workforce about what the changes heralded.

Today there is a much more open attitude to change, both from the point of view of management – which wants change to keep the business alive to the real world – and employees – who want the opportunity to embrace change and prosper from it. Of course, there may still be resistance to change if it is poorly communicated and managed. The answer is to foster an atmosphere where the idea of change is a constant and welcomed element.

When people make suggestions for change they should always be listened to, and their suggestions acted on if appropriate. The ability of people to generate ideas is unlimited. The problem is that the skill of management is not. This is the reason consultants do so well. A consultant's primary role is to listen to what people have to say and to feed this back to management.

Information and communications technology will develop so rapidly in the next twenty years that unless organisations foster a welcoming atmosphere for change they will be left far behind those that do.

A learning environment

Learning is a constant and continuous aspect of life. There is always something to learn. This is true for individuals, teams, and organisations. A learning environment is one where learning is encouraged, both in terms of its acquisition and its application. This leads in turn to a process of transformation.

There is nothing more frustrating than to learn something and then be prevented from exploring the application of that learning. It does not matter where the learning comes from. It is possible to learn from superiors, staff, colleagues, customers, suppliers – anyone, in fact. But this learning will happen only if awareness is maintained and opportunities to learn are exploited.

Perhaps the best way to learn is to listen, to ask for clarity, and to consciously acknowledge what is being learnt.

- Not knowing that you know – is *wisdom.*
- Knowing that you do not know – is *intelligence.*
- Knowing that you know – is *arrogance.*
- Thinking that you know when you do not – is *foolishness.*

2.3 Flat structures

Hierarchical organisation structures have typically been represented by a triangle.

Figure 2.1 Hierarchical structure

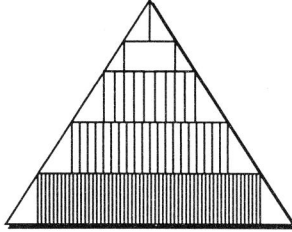

Communication in such structures flows up and down the lines of command. Each part of the hierarchy functions independently, with some cross-connections at appropriate levels. This kind of structure has worked well for hundreds of years, but is now obsolete.

Flat structures operate by coordinating the efforts of business process and project teams with a simple reporting link to the coordinating executive. Heads of the various teams communicate and meet as necessary, and there is much cross-fertilisation of ideas between teams. A flat structure might be drawn as follows.

Figure 2.2 Flat structure

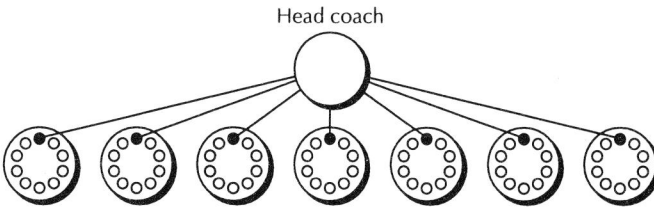

Head coach

The role of teams in flat structures

Earlier in this chapter you read about business process and project teams as part of a structure based on cooperation and teamwork. It is this team approach which underlies the idea of the flat structure.

Imagine an organisation made up of twenty teams. Each team has its coach, and there is a head coach who oversees the work of the team coaches. The head coach may have support staff, but their role is to support the head coach, not to interfere with the work of the team coaches.

Each team in this structure knows what it has to do. Each team will have a single purpose: to satisfy customers, to produce a high-quality product or a reliable information systems infrastructure, or whatever. The eventual profit targets of the organisation will be the outcome of each team achieving its purpose.

In this way the flat structure provides all the ingredients for releasing the diversity and creativity of its people, and by so doing can achieve considerable success.

Span of authority

In the traditional form of hierarchical management the four key management activities were seen to be:

- planning;
- organising;
- directing; and
- controlling.

In such an environment it was desirable to limit the manager's span of authority to a handful of people. A total of six or eight people was considered to be the most a manager could effectively 'control'. Today the roles of managers are changing and people are expected to take greater responsibility for their own actions. The manager's key activities today are:

- envisioning;
- co-ordinating;
- coaching;
- supporting.

In this new arrangement of activities the manager can work directly with a larger group of people, and so flatter organisations are not only possible but make the approach to 'freedom with responsibility' more real and effective.

In these flatter environments decisions are taken much lower down in the organisation, authority is shared and decision conferences are arranged so that people can participate in the decision-making process. Sharing authority and working cooperatively are the key elements of success in the flatter structures of the future.

2.4 Decision support

There is a clear link between information and decision-making. In open management and with flat structures decisions become team-based. Information systems must support the work of the teams.

The team coaches will be the owners of their team's system and they will endeavour to ensure that the system reflects the needs of the team. Taking the example of the 'customer satisfaction team', an information system will be needed that operates on the current needs of customers. The customer name will be the key, and inputting the customer's name would call up a history of the customer's business, the current state of orders, and any indebtedness. If the customer had not ordered recently it would also show data on when they were last contacted, and so on. The focus of the system would be the customer.

It is still possible from such a system to get data on total value of orders and deliveries, by product, customer class, etc. The data can still be manipulated to suit current decision needs. This is what decision support is all about.

Decision support is about supporting those making the decisions (the teams) with systems which they can use to provide the information that they want. This can be done by individuals in the team, but it is more likely to be a team effort, with members of the team sharing the information and agreeing action. This has the advantage of producing a range of opinions and ideas about the interpretation of the information. This is where diversity and creativity is so important. Each member of the team will have his own specific skills and talent to bring, but it is when the team works in harmony and with flair that results are achieved. It is this harmony that the decision support system is trying to support.

Automated administration

Business administration has a primary role of collecting data for every single business transaction and maintaining a record of its occurrence and value to the business. This has for a long time been synonymous with 'keeping the books'. It is a task which can be easily automated. Of course, it goes beyond simply providing basic business records and into the realms of providing instant management feedback.

There are four aspects of automated administration of importance to our discussion of information management.

- *Processing data as it happens*
  Processing transactions as they occur eliminates delay and allows management to be more responsive to what is happening. Not only is the processing smoother and simpler, but management information can be updated in a continuous flow. Electronic point of sale (EPOS) is a good example of this approach, as is just-in-time (JIT) materials management. The requirements are simply a device at the point where the transaction data originates and a system to input it to.

  The results can be presented graphically with great effect. Imagine a cash-flow system processing data every time a cheque is issued and received. The display shows a 'thermometer' on the screen, with a red bar moving up and down to reflect the cash as it flows in and out.

  Business does not stand still, it is a continuous flow – so why should we try to represent it with monthly or weekly snapshots when we can produce a moving video of events?

- *Continuous planning and performance monitoring*
  We can then adopt a process of continuous planning and monitoring for whatever period is deemed appropriate for the organisation. Current information on what is happening is compared with the most recent forecasts. This is then used to change future plans, and to influence understanding of what is happening in the marketplace.

  Variance analysis is used as an automated way of signalling areas for attention – not on a weekly or monthly basis, but on the shortest possible meaningful time interval. This can increase the speed and effectiveness of business controls.

▪ *Trends and probabilities*
With data flowing in as events occur it becomes possible to look at the way events are moving – the business trends; not what happened last month, but what is happening today. From this it is possible to calculate trends and to amend them with the latest data. Business models can be used to anticipate what is to be, rather than to study what has been. Correcting past mistakes is nowhere near as good as avoiding future ones.

▪ *Information to decision points*
With information systems that are being updated continuously it is possible to feed decision-making information as it arises to the decision points where it is needed. If significant changes have occurred against expectations a signal can be flashed on-screen to interrupt whatever else might be happening, or a message can be left in the user's e-mail box. All this can be automated, but only if the dataflows, datastreams, and decision points of the business have been defined.

Information explosion

It has been noted that, in spite of technological advances, there seems to be more paper flying around than ever before. The Royal Mail handles more letters and has had to spend millions of pounds on automation to cope with the deluge of paper. Scanners and document imaging are vital parts of most computer systems as we attempt to cope with the paperwork by putting it into the system.

Databases have expanded enormously and now include images, graphics and video clips as well as data. Not long ago, storage capacity might have been 16k, 32k or 64k: we now talk in terms of megabytes (one million bytes) and gigabytes (1,000 million bytes). The sheer scale of information storage leads to an attitude that everything can be stored; there is no longer any need to be selective. This then leads to two problems:

▪ knowing what information is useful; and
▪ being able to access what is required.

When the required information has been identified, getting it can be quite a process. Database management systems and report-writing software can help, as can executive information systems. But searching for the pertinent needle of fact in the haystack of information still presents management with a problem.

Sales trends

The sales manager was discussing the need for daily information on sales trends. The management accountant had offered a daily report on sales which would be extracted from the sales accounting system based on invoices raised the previous day. The sales manager commented that it was approximately two weeks between an order coming in and an invoice being raised. 'But a sale doesn't take place until the invoice is raised,' the management accountant said.

The northern region sales-team leader said that his people considered that they had made a sale when they took the order, so that perhaps an analysis of the day's orders would be a better indication of sales trends than the invoice data. 'And of course,' added the marketing manager 'we can provide the latest projections based on current sales extrapolated using the market trend data that we have.'

'So that's three types of sales trend information that I can get,' the sales manager said. 'Which is the most relevant for me to feed through to production scheduling?'

2.1 The right information

Based on the scenario given above, which information would you give to production scheduling, and why?

2.5 The new view of productivity

In his book, *The Empty Raincoat*, Charles Handy refers to a new formula for productivity:

$$\frac{1}{2} \times 2 \times 3 = P$$

This translates as: half the people working twice as hard for twice the pay, producing three times the output, equals performance and profit. This is certainly the way that many large organisations approach productivity.

Reports of large organisations making significant profit increases while laying off thousands of people can be seen every day in the press. But this is an artificial form of productivity because the equation does not recognise that organisations depend on consumers for their profit, and the unemployed are not good consumers. In turn, the state – i.e. taxpayers – has to carry the social cost burden of this policy in the form of increased taxes to pay the unemployed. This, in turn, affects our ability as consumers. In due course, this policy leads to a slowing down of growth, and then to recession. The fact that information systems are supporting this new view of productivity, and will continue to do so, will drive us to the point where one group of people working very hard has a lot of money but no time to enjoy it. Another group will have little money and all the time in the world.

Perhaps an alternative formula for long-term productivity and prosperity would be:

$$2 \times \frac{1}{2} \times 3 = P$$

which translates as: twice as many people working half as much for half the pay, producing three times as much, equals profit and prosperity.

More consumers with more money is much more beneficial overall than a few consumers with a lot. And this is the way that some organisations are heading, with part-time workers and contract workers and only a few core staff. We shall have to wait and see which approach works best in the long run.

2.6 Summary

- Access to information opens the door to new freedoms and responsibilities. It demands a new approach to management which fully recognises people's rights and differences.
- New, flatter management structures will emerge.
- Decision support is about access to information and dealing with events 'as they happen'.
- Will we go for $\frac{1}{2} \times 2 \times 3 = P$, or for $2 \times \frac{1}{2} \times 3 = P$?

3 Employment and People

In the last twenty years the world of work has changed radically. The switch from manual effort to mental effort has changed the whole basis of what is done, and of the way in which it is done. Most of this change has been brought about by information technology. In Britain we still operate under an obsolete work ethic that was espoused during the industrial revolution and which continues to bedevil attitudes to employment. This must change.

3.1 The things we do

The workforce of Britain today is split evenly between men and women. The majority of the unemployed are men who can, by and large, offer only manual skills – which are no longer needed in our highly mechanised and automated society. There has been a major shift from physical effort to mental effort. The demand today is for information workers.

The emphasis in the workplace today is in six areas:

- extension of mechanisation and automation;
- maintenance of machines;
- design;
- programming systems;
- information handling; and
- providing services.

Extension of mechanisation and automation

In all areas of manufacturing the processes of converting raw materials into finished product are largely mechanised and automated. *Making* things has changed into *assembling* things made by machines, and even this assembly process is being increasingly automated. This process of change will continue, because machines are easier to manage, do not tire or argue, and produce high-quality products at high speed.

Not only have the machining operations been automated, but so has production planning and control. Computers now schedule work through the factory and coordinate the supply of materials to the machines. The aim is to balance production flow and increase productivity, which computers do very well.

There are some traditional areas of work which still have a large component of physical/manual skills. Construction and civil engineering, furniture-making and shoe manufacture, are examples. But even in these areas, if it can be done by machines it is – or soon will be.

Maintenance of machines

The machines that now manufacture have to be kept working. They need to be 'tended' by people who keep them oiled and cleaned and replace worn parts. This process of continuous maintenance is a vital element of the modern factory. Even the machine operators of a few years ago have found their role changed to one of 'minding' the machines rather than operating them.

The operation of the machines is now automated and takes the form of computer programs fed into control mechanisms. Just as the computer-controlled washing machine can run a complete program from a simple selection dial, so the modern machine tools can turn out complex components within extremely fine tolerances.

Programming systems

Of course, the programs have to be produced in the first place. This is where the mental effort now comes in. Instead of producing the components or setting the machines a program is written which instructs the machine what to do.

This will include the feeding of raw materials onto the work surface of the machine. The machine programmer uses a computer to produce the program by feeding in design data such as machining angles, depths, coordinates, etc. The computer then changes this data into the digital language that the machine has been built to respond to. The machine programmer is able to do this from the information provided by the product designer, and sometimes, if computer-aided design (CAD) has been used, the machine programming can also be automated.

Design

Design is a growth area in the new world of work. It is here that the ideas for new products are transformed from ideas into possibilities. The role of design goes beyond the usual concept of the way something looks, to the essential details of how it works and how can be built. Design teams need to consist of people with a diverse range of skills, so that what starts out as a vision can be converted into cost-effective reality.

CAD is now a principal tool for designers. It can take basic outlines drawn on a pad, or directly on the screen with a mouse, and produce three-dimensional images that can be moved about and changed on the screen. These designs can be converted into the basic mathematics needed for subsequent manufacture and checked for reality. Step by step the product is designed until it is finally agreed.

Information handling

When people sit at their computer terminals, whatever they are doing – from CAD, through JIT to word processing – they are handling information. Information handling means inputting data into a computer system to cause some subsequent effect on a process and/or activity. Whether the information will be used to produce a component, control a material delivery system, or produce the front page of today's newspaper, it is still information handling.

Information handling calls for a variety of skills, which include the operation of the computer system, mouse, keyboard, etc. Most importantly, they include the knowledge of the effect the data will have, and an understanding of the systems involved and the implications of what they are doing. This is why information handlers are often referred to as 'knowledge workers'. The information system is, in effect, simply a way of transferring the operative's knowledge into the system so that it produces the desired results.

Providing services

In the last 50 years there has been a migration of workers from manufacturing industry to the provision of services. One of the fastest growth areas in Britain during these 50 years has been tourism. This is almost entirely a service industry concerned with transporting, accommodating, feeding and entertaining people. That it uses information systems extensively is to be expected, but the main factors that tourists are aware of are those supplied directly by people.

The second largest area of growth has been in the personal services sector, which includes all those services needed in the home – from window cleaning to motor-car maintenance – and those needed by the individual – from hairdressing to eating out. Many of these services are provided successfully without the use of information systems, except to the extent that they are used to administer the services provided.

3.2 The way we do things

So if the things that are done have been changing rapidly, what about the way in which they are done? These have changed as well, and in so many ways that it is hard to give any specific guidance on the scope and extent of these changes. Perhaps the best approach is to provide a few scenarios.

Writing on the keyboard

Date: 1984 TJ always wrote using a fountain pen and had his draft typed by his secretary on her word processor. He then edited the draft and returned it to her for final typing. TJ had his own machine but avowed that he couldn't write on it, maintaining that it didn't have the same creative feeling as his pen and paper.

Date: 1998 TJ writes on his machine. He can work just as fast and as creatively on his keyboard as with his pen. He no longer has a secretary – or needs one. His writing has improved, it flows better and he is able to decide the layout he wants to use. He also has the advantages of an on-line spellchecker and a thesaurus.

Direct banking

TJ has visited his bank once in the last three years, having done all his business using telephone, fax, and mail. This type of banking has been possible in principle for many years, but now when TJ contacts them they are able to get his details on the screen immediately, ask for his password combination and then process his request. The fact that his account is with a branch in Yorkshire and he lives in Gloucestershire is beside the point.

TJ's only physical contact with his bank is in withdrawing cash from the cash machine, and he uses very little cash because he is well supplied with plastic.

Presenting information

Working as a consultant TJ needs, from time to time, to make presentations to his clients. He used to do this entirely with overhead or slide projectors and carefully prepared printed notes.

Today he can present to most of his clients using a PC, and if necessary some form of screen projection. He can use animated graphics, speech, music, video and text. He can put together a presentation on his computer, edit it and then present it. He can record what he has presented and produce a printed version of it if needed.

When equipment is not available he uses a printed set of documents from his system, which he goes through with clients as if he was using the PC. The effect is always good.

In fact, TJ's information systems are his second most important tool, after his brain. He doesn't have a particularly sophisticated set of equipment: a PC, a word processor, a matrix printer and a bubble-jet printer, a fax and an answering machine. He work with clients all over the world. Ten years ago, he did most of the things he does today, but today he does most of them quite differently.

3.3 The human–computer interface

Today, and increasingly in the future, people acquiring systems are going to expect a high-quality human–computer interface (HCI). Ease of use and ease of learning will become key selling points for the software of the future.

So what constitutes a good HCI? A good HCI is based on four underlying principles: clarity, consistency, common sense and comfort. These four principles should be applied with rigour in the four key areas of HCI:

* working environment;
* system appearance;
* user support; and
* interaction.

Working environment

The working environment includes all the physical aspects of the system: the equipment, the workplace, seating, lighting, and contact with others, e.g. customers. These are all important and have to be carefully designed to ensure that the four principles of HCI are applied. Imagine a situation where different software packages running on the same workstation demanded different uses of the keyboard and the mouse. This would obviously be very confusing for users.

The incidence of repetitive strain injury (RSI) is increasing, mainly due to the growing use of computer keyboards and mice. This serious and debilitating condition is caused by inflammation of the sheaths that carry the tendons that control our finger movements. This in turn is mainly caused by using keyboards at the wrong height. People suffer with sore shoulders and stiff necks because their screens are in the wrong position.

Failure to address these basic ergonomic factors will have a serious effect on the efficiency with which people interface with the system. It is hard to be effective when uncomfortable and/or in pain.

System appearance

This is sometimes referred to as screen design, but it is far more than this. Appearance has to do with what users see when they experience the system. At present the primary view users have of the system is through the screen. This is their 'window' on the system and sometimes it presents a very dismal view indeed.

There is a considerable amount of effort involved in getting the appearance of the system to meet the four principles – clarity, consistency, common sense and comfort. Some of the factors are screen layout, menus, colour, sequence of data fields, message display, use of multi-windows, font size and type, use of upper and lower case text, headings, screen relationships, navigation within and between screens, etc.

To achieve clarity it is also helpful to think of simplicity and to keep the view users have of the system as simple as possible. This enables users to find what they want and to carry out actions simply and easily.

User support

One of the most frustrating aspects of coputer systems is the level of system support offered – usually very little. And, if the user requests help from the system, it is frequently unavailable. Some systems have a convoluted approach to the use of the keys, for which the user needs a long thin card, which he positions on top of the keyboard.

Three levels of support are essential.

- The most important provides messages that help the user to do things right. These are not the same as error messages, which tell him what he has done wrong.
- The second is the help requested when the user becomes stuck. This should ask him what he wants to know, then give him the answer – or at least offer a list of possibilities to choose from. And either of these should be in the context of how he is using the system.
- The third will be in the form of general information about the system being used, and how maximum benefit can be obtained from it.

Interaction

A computer user should be able to predict exactly what will happen each time he interacts with the system. Interaction has many aspects, but perhaps the most important are:

- positive responses;
- protective responses; and
- supportive responses.

Positive responses are always encouraging. They explain what is being done and how it could be done more effectively.

Protective responses warn that something is about to be done and ask for confirmation before proceeding. This helps the user to avoid unintentional errors – such as deleting the wrong file.

Supportive responses give guidance and help the user to proceed through the work being undertaken.

Windows, icons and mice

The use of the mouse and windows has become a major factor in the design of HCI. The three elements involved are

- a pointer, usually an arrow head on the screen, which is moved around the screen using a hand-held device called a mouse;

- symbols (icons), usually positioned around the edges of the screen; and
- windows that display information related to the icon selected.

The primary objective of using a mouse is to make the interaction between user and computer easier. In most cases this is exactly what happens, but there are a growing number of examples where programmers have been carried away and the sheer range of options has become confusing. In addition, screen layout can become cluttered if too many icons are used. Here is a wonderful example of a good idea being destroyed by overzealous use in the hands of people who do not understand how to apply it.

There is a great deal more to improving the human–computer interface than using icons instead of words, and mice instead of keyboards. The simplification of any aspect of the use of computers is a good thing, but when good ideas are applied badly, and then built into such systems as executive information systems, the worst side of information technology is shown.

Every new idea offers opportunities to make the human–computer interface better than ever, but the information technicians must not get carried away with their own enthusiasm. There is a well-known saying: 'It is easy to make things difficult, but difficult to make things easy'.

Multimedia

Multimedia is one of those aspects of information technology which fits everywhere. At home, at work, in the high street, travelling, wherever – in future there will be screens and user devices (keyboards, mice, microphones, touch screens) which allow interaction, via the new data superhighways, with vast stores of information.

These stores of information will be offered via voice, music, video, graphics and text, and will allow the user to mix these, browse for what is available, access other systems (via client/server links), make phone calls, send faxes and so on.

The separation recognised today between TV, telephones, fax, computer, audio equipment, etc., will disappear. The trend already exists in multi-service telephones (fax, answerphone, phone, photocopier).

These new multimedia systems will be used for learning, working, banking, shopping, entertainment, communication, organising activities and so on. And, as miniaturisation goes even further, this will all be accessible from our completely mobile laptop system with built-in personal network connector working via satellite. The sky really is the limit.

3.4 The psychology of technology

Of course, there is no such thing as the 'psychology of technology', but the heading serves to highlight the simple fact that technology has a powerful effect on the psychology of those who come into close contact with it, and this means most of us. Let us examine three key aspects of the psychological impact of technology:

- the fear or apprehension common amongst users ('technofear');
- interactivity or the lack of it; and
- a question of control.

Technofear

'Technofear' is caused by five psychological factors.

- *Fear of the unknown.* All humans fear the unknown, to varying degrees. This fear is based on the anticipation that all might not be well, that there might be some disturbance to their comfort or security, physical or mental.
- *Self-doubt.* From birth we are given incorrect information about ourselves. Much of this information is negative. We are told that we are stupid, we are naughty, we look a mess, our hair is too long, and so on. This builds a strong negative self-attitude which, in the face of a challenge, can lead these negative thoughts to surface and cause self-doubt and an inability to cope.
- *Fear of ridicule.* We all have a strong sense of belonging. This is reflected in a need for peer acceptance. This acceptance is important, and to be accepted we have to be equal or similar to our peers. To be different generates ridicule, and could lead to rejection and isolation.
- *Negative motivation.* To carry out any activity we need to be motivated. This motivation can be either positive – 'I want to do it' – or negative – 'I do not want to do it but will to get it out of the way'. Negative motivation leads to the minimum necessary action and is an obstacle to learning.
- *Fear of failure and censure* – There is a widespread perception that failure is a sign of weakness, and will lead to ridicule or worse. A very challenging changing environment increases the fear of failure and consequent censure. So many people are hesitant about trying new things in case they fail.

Interactivity or the lack of it

Contact between individuals will consist of actions and reactions – the two-way process of *interaction*. First-time computer users have a tendency to expect some similar two-way contact. Unfortunately the vast majority of systems do not operate this way. They have been designed and programmed to provide a certain level of functionality and this they do, come what may. It is not generally possible to expect the system to interact. The very best that can be expected is some response to the user's action. If the user proceeds within the confines of the system's functionality it will respond appropriately. If not, then a cryptic message will be generated to alert the user that he is on the wrong track.

There are systems which are designed to interact. These are built with interaction as their functionality. They are mainly systems to aid learning, and are given the generic title of computer-based training (CBT). The interaction here is still programmed, but there is much more of what can be loosely called dialogue. Choices are offered, and the user has some freedom in how to proceed through the system. Help and support are available.

Expert systems also offer a form of interaction. Once again they are programmed to operate in a certain way, usually to request some information, and based on it to offer suggestions for action. They can provide information on how they arrived at the suggestions, and the user can add more information and see where it leads. But true random interaction will have to be left to people.

A question of control

Users are always in control in that they can switch the computer off. They can change data, delete data and add data, provided that they have the appropriate authority levels. So why is there a question of control?

The question exists because when a user enters into a system to take some action he has no choice but to follow the prescribed path of the programmer – even if this is a clumsy and time-consuming method. Sometimes an alternative is offered which leads to quicker results, but this is usually through some remembered sequence of keys. Once entered into a system the user sacrifices control over how he does things to the system's program. This can be both frustrating and annoying.

The graphics nightmare

TJ – a fairly experienced computer user – started to use a system that he was unfamiliar with. An on-line tutorial was offered to help him become familiar with the system. He started the program and was prompted: 'Please enter your name'. He did so, and the next screen said, 'Hello TJ'.

He attempted to move on but nothing happened, so he waited. He was then presented with a series of graphical displays explaining each icon and indicating the functionality they offered in the system. Apparently, he was supposed to remember all of this. There seemed to be no way to skip to the material that interested him, nor any way to exit except from the whole system. There was no menu from which to select.

TJ exited the system, then set it up again and started to explore the help facility. This was much more practical and useful. But what he did learn very quickly was that this was a system very definitely in control.

3.5 Humane information management

It is important to understand the basic purpose and direction of information management. Four headings will help:

- information is for *people* to use;
- *people* need support to do their jobs;
- technology is inherently unfriendly to *people*;
- recognise the roles *people* have and construct information systems to help them.

Information is for people to use

People make decisions. At the very best, information systems can make suggestions. Automated systems can respond to pre-programmed rules in a mechanical way, but this is not really decision-making. Setting the rules is the decision-making and it is done by people. Information systems, then, are the servant of people, not vice versa.

For people to make effective use of information it has to be:

- available when they want it;
- in a form they understand;
- reliable;
- adaptable;
- current.

People need support to do their jobs

Information systems can support people in their work by providing information, but also by:

- allowing easy communication;
- allowing them to share information with others;
- providing easy to learn systems;
- providing tools for data manipulation;
- providing simple on-line and off-line guides for using systems.

If people are supported effectively in their use of systems they will use them more effectively and in turn those people will be more effective. Performance is determined partly by ability, partly by confidence, partly by events, and partly by support: remove any of these elements and performance suffers.

Technology is unfriendly to people

The term 'user friendly technology' is a misnomer. Technology is not friendly. It is cold, clinical, inflexible, demanding and controlling. The best that can be done is to create a human–computer interface which is as humane as possible. It will still not be friendly. Recognising this fact might help to stop programmers trying to make them friendly, using ridiculous graphics sequences.

In future it might be possible to construct systems which give a semblance of friendliness. It will certainly help when the user can talk to them, but it will depend on what they say in return.

Recognise the roles people have and construct information systems to help them

Information systems should reflect and adapt to the roles that users have to adopt when they are working. These roles will usually consist of activities and tasks that have to be carried out. At this level, information systems can be very powerful by providing specific functions to help with each task. Further, the system could be designed so that, by defining the tasks to be performed, the system can organise the functionality required out of its library of functions. It could also gather the information required to use these functions. This means that every individual could have a tailor-made system to support them in their job. This would be a truly effective performance support system.

These kinds of developments are within sight. It is to be hoped that, as they arise, the needs of *people* are given priority.

3.6 Human information processors

The human brain is a very complex and sophisticated information processor. It is more powerful and has more capacity then the largest computers yet produced. That we use only a small percentage of this capacity – believed to be between two and three per cent – is not important. What is important is that we process information in a particular way, and though similar, this varies for each of us. In addition, the signals we receive will make sense to us only in relation to the situation we are in when we receive them.

The human information processor has five sensory mechanisms for picking up and inputting data: sight, hearing, touch, taste and smell. These sensory mechanisms are linked to the brain so that as data is 'sensed' it is interpreted by comparison with knowledge of past experience and understanding of our world – the individual world that we each inhabit. A meaning is assigned to the sensory data and the body reacts according to the assigned meaning.

The first key to efficiency in the human information processor is to have all sensory mechanisms at work and to be 'sensory aware' of what is being picked up. The second key is to have the knowledge, experience and understanding of the local environment so that appropriate meanings can be assigned to these signals and appropriate action taken.

Sometimes the signals we receive can be distorted by 'noise' either in the ambiguity of the way the message is constructed or in the literal sense of a 'noisy' line. If it is unable to assign meanings to the signals being picked up, the brain endeavours to discover meanings through exploration, experiment and questioning. When meanings are discovered, action is taken and the results of that action monitored. If satisfactory, those meanings are stored as being a relevant interpretation of the signals; the information base has been expanded. This is the process called 'learning'.

People are largely unaware of these processes taking place and rely on their brains to 'get on with it'. Some rely more heavily on the brain's left hemisphere, which processes data in an analytical and logical way; some rely on the right hemisphere, which processes data in an intuitive, visual way. This is why some managers appreciate columns of figures and others appreciate graphs. However it is done, the outcome is either an assigned meaning or confusion. Sometimes, rather than admitting the confusion, people assign meanings that do not make sense – as if they have made a random choice of meanings. It is far better to admit confusion and to seek clarity than to forge ahead on randomly assigned meanings. Sometimes the meanings assigned come from old messages that have been implanted in the brain – what is referred to as 'prejudice'.

The more an individual has learnt and the more open he is to learning, the more effective he is as a human information processor. In desensitising the brain – for example by not listening – the brain's efficiency is reduced and the learning process halted – it is as if the same meanings are automatically attributed to information received from the environment.

Even the most sophisticated management information system can only feed the senses with information. Appropriate meanings for this information must be sought constantly before action is taken, and in doing this the human information processor grows and develops.

The assimilation and understanding of information received is the first part of human information processing. The second part is the way understanding is disseminated to others (communication) or choices made (decision-making).

An efficient human information processor will be able to organise and file information received in such a way that it can be accessed and enhanced (i.e. learning takes place). Sometimes when information is provided by the system, it is unnecessary to store it, so the human information processor becomes a 'system operator' rather than a 'knowledge worker'.

The final stage of the process is the output stage: the provision of information and advice to others – which is especially important when the 'others' are customers. The advantage of the human information processor over the system is that he can respond to questions and interact with other human information processors so as to enhance understanding. Information systems can often be frustrating precisely because they lack this interactivity and responsiveness. Systems are good at providing access to information, but not yet good at helping people to understand the information or to make choices.

3.7 Summary

- The things we do and the way in which we do them are changing rapidly in many ways, particularly in relation to working with IM.
- The way that people interact with information systems – especially multimedia – is a critical factor of effectiveness and enjoyment. The human–computer interface is becoming a vital ingredient of success.
- There are psychological aspects to changes that are happening, and the extent to which people feel they are or are not in control.
- By focusing on people and what they need it is possible that *humane* information processors can be produced.
- People are 'human information processors': the success with which they do this can impact on the overall quality and integrity of the MIS.

4 New Connections

4.1 Getting connected

Being informed is about being able to get the right information when it is required. Information management is partly about providing access to the information that managers want, and being connected is one way – perhaps in days to come the only way – of accessing such information.

Getting connected may mean being linked to other parts of the organisation via its organisation's local-area network (LAN) or wide-area network (WAN). These in-house networks enable colleagues to share common facilities and data resources, and are configured to meet the specific business needs of the organisation and use the organisation's own technology. Such organisation-based networks have to date provided an excellent way of accessing databases and of using decision support services (DSS) and executive information systems (EIS). However, the world of communications is changing rapidly and managers are increasingly using the Internet.

The Internet opens up the possibilities of the World Wide Web (the web) for a wide range of information, although at the moment around 90 per cent of Internet use is for e-mail. Connection is also possible via your organisation's own intranet, which, although private, can provide links to the Internet.

4.2 The Internet

The Internet – a vast network of inter-linked computers – is accessed via a modem and a telephone line. The Internet is not 'owned' by any organisation, nor can it be switched off. It is, in fact, the method by which computers communicate with each other. In order to connect to the Internet it is necessary to connect a home or work PC or workstation to one of these computers or client servers. This is effected by subscribing to a particular provider, via whose computer links can be made to the Internet and to other computers. A subscription fee is paid and the provider of the telecommunications link (phone line) charges for time on-line. Although the main use of the Internet is e-mail, there are many more things that can be done. Potentially most promising, perhaps, is access to the World Wide Web, also known as the web, or WWW.

The web is not a network as such, but provides a vast range of linked documents – referred to as *pages* – held in locations (computers) where information is stored and accessed via the Internet. The web makes use of the Internet more practical and interesting because it is possible to store text, pictures and video for transmission over the Internet to the user's computer.

LIVERPOOL
JOHN MOORES UNIVERSITY
AVRIL ROBARTS LRC
TEL. 0151 231 4022

The primary purpose of the web is for web-site owners to provide information and advertising, with a view to making direct sales of their products and services.

The owners of web sites are developing sophisticated interactive offerings to attract people to stay at their site. It seems that visitors soon tire of 'passive' pages.

Internet addresses

To use the Internet it is necessary to sign on with a service provider and register an *address*. This address allows computers on the Internet to know where to send the information selected by the user. The address is, in fact, a storage place on the computer used by your service provider.

An address consists of a user identification (ID) and the address of the computer. For example, the CompuServe service has the address

compuserve.com

The user ID sits in front of this address, together with the symbol '@' (meaning 'at'). So the author's office address at the Executive Transformation Company is:

etcoffice@compuserve.com

Web addresses are longer than the e-mail addresses, such as the one above, and operate to identify the web site. It is necessary to use an e-mail address when a web site is visited only if information is being collected ('downloaded') or if follow-up contact is being requested.

Browsing the web

To search for information on the web it is possible to enter the full web-site page address or URL (uniform resource locator), or to click on a link in an existing page. This is done using a *web browser*, a piece of software that provides an on-screen interface and which usually contains a *home page* from which searches can be inititated, using key words or by clicking on links.

There are a number of web browsers available, some of which are provided as components of the Internet service. CompuServe provides *Microsoft Internet Explorer* which automatically brings the home page on-screen when the Internet button is clicked. From this home page, the user can either go direct to a desired web page by entering the page number, can ask for a search by keywords, or click on one of the preset buttons available.

In CompuServe, for example, there are many facilities available from within the CompuServe network, without accessing the Internet. These services include forums (bulletin boards), chat links and news. Of course, there is much more via the Internet.

e-mail

The largest single use of the Internet is for e-mail. The creation and transmission of messages and attached files is very easy, and modern e-mail facilities offered by service providers such as CompuServe are very simple to use. A good e-mail facility will contain an address book, a range of message files, a facility to reply to a message, off-line creation of messages to send at a later time, file attachment and an ability to create groups of addresses for multiple transmission of messages.

The beauty of e-mail is that the user needs to be on-line only to send and collect mail. Once downloaded to the computer it can be edited, printed or otherwise processed. Electronic mail is rapidly becoming one of the main forms of business communication, via both the Internet and internal *intranets*.

4.3 Intranets

The Internet has come in-house. The creation of intranets – closed private communities limited to the organisational boundaries – has much to commend it. Intranets will transform the nature of information dissemination and access for those companies that make the moderate investment to reconfigure their LANs and WANs as intranets. Care has to be taken that systems which need to be constantly connected – order processing, for example – stay off the intranet, otherwise the *bandwidth* needed will be significant.

The conversion of LANs to intranets requires the addition of web servers and switches and the use of hypertext mark-up language (HTML) to create the web pages. Appropriate experts should be consulted for advice on the action required, because this is a relatively new technology – and, even though it uses the same devices as the Internet, it has to fit in with the needs of the business. The infrastructure that is created is, of course, only part of the story. The remainder concerns what the intranet is to be used for.

Possible uses include:

- e-mail in all its forms;
- performance information particular to the specific activities of a given manager, held on database and continuously updated as events progress;
- intranet pages with the latest market and product update information;
- news and information of general background interest;
- discussion groups – could take place on-line and be joined by anyone with an interest in contributing to the debate;
- on-line decision conferences;
- bulletin boards on particular topics of interest within the organisation.

The extent of information access could go outside the organisation if the intranet was connected to the Internet. If this route is followed, a secure interface – usually referred to as 'firewall software' – will be required. This uses security clearance criteria for those wishing to pass through, either from outside to inside or vice versa. This is useful for widely dispersed organisations that wish to use the Internet for communicating between sites without having to incur the expense of a WAN for e-mail. Intranets are also useful for organisations with different user platforms, e.g. PCs and Macintosh.

Once an appropriate intranet has been built it provides all the facilities of the Internet, but in a way that directly serves the needs of the business. If its bandwidth permits, the intranet could include full multimedia presentations. Care must be taken not to clog the system, however, or e-mail will soon become snail-mail.

If the right balance is struck, an intranet can provide a range of practical and valuable services that include communication, information retrieval, information search and group working.

Communication is provided by familiar facilities: e-mail and bulletin boards/ forums where information, questions and opinions are posted and can attract responses from those interested enough to pay a visit. In addition, it is now possible to broadcast information to all system users or to selected groups, and a user can signal on-screen that his mailbox is active.

Information retrieval is facilitated by the creation of web-site equivalents that contain the latest information on a wide range of topics. Users can visit the sites that interest them and download information as appropriate to use in their work. In this way windows are opened on information on customers, results, technical information, personnel information (e.g. job vacancies) – the possibilities are endless.

Information search has become an important feature of the Internet and can be equally useful on an intranet as the number of internal sites grows and the information held therein expands. Group work is also greatly facilitated by an intranet. People working on the same project, or with the same customer, can share the site containing the workgroup's information and get updates on events. Such sites might need to be protected using passwords so that they are open only to members of the work group.

The intranet, then, is a means for people to travel through the organisation's information infrastructure and to find windows onto the particular information they want. However, there are difficulties to be overcome in creating a truly effective intranet. These can be classed as either *technical/structural* or *content/usage*.

Technical/structural difficulties have to do with the creation of the intranet and the provision of the servers, switches and cabling necessary to support the size and capability of the system required. Many LANs are configured with standard cables, which means that the bandwidth is unlikely to support multimedia without a considerable degradation in the process. 'Browsing' will be very slow. The need is for optic-fibre cables, so that the intranet can be truly responsive and carry a wide range of information media. Appropriate software will also be needed.

Content/usage difficulties stem from the design of the intranet procedures and the way that access is controlled, as well as the creation and maintenance of the various sites. A site manager should be appointed to look after the number and design of sites, as well as the security levels attached to sites. In this way the content can be managed and a record of usefulness maintained by recording 'hits' on sites, indicating those which are popular and those which are not. The site manager can also ensure that the sites created support business effort rather than provide game opportunities for staff, although some play might be available at certain times.

Sites can also have links to other sites or to databases from where information can be collected on request. Such links have to be created and managed, and could include links to sites on the Internet for stock-market data, newspaper abstracting services, etc. The scope and capability of intranets is only now being explored and, as technology develops, will become more extensive and potentially more useful.

4.4 Traffic control

Making the best use of intranet and Internet will depend on the way that the data highways are kept open and free-moving. This is perhaps one of the thorniest questions of the whole network scene.

The main element of the networking infrastructure is the 'server'. This piece of computer equipment is crucial to successful networks, particularly in the way in which it organises and manages the particular needs of the group that it serves. Servers can be seen as traffic controllers.

One way to look at the work of servers is to imagine a car journey. The driver has a good idea of the best route to follow and sets out to do this. However, on reaching a certain junction he finds a diversion – so another route is needed. Some time later as he approaches his destination he hears on the radio that the town is congested owing to peak-hour traffic volumes, so he decides to pull into a service station and have a break and a cup of tea. After some time, he decides to check the state of the traffic via the local RAC information terminal, and discovers that it is now flowing. He decides to continue his journey.

The same principle applies to networks: the server does all the work, receiving and despatching data at very high speeds – all over the world in the case of the Internet, or all over the organisation in the case of the intranet. Local servers usually also have the capacity to store data until it is asked for and to configure and format it for individual workstations.

Servers make the networks that we have been talking about truly effective. Without servers, i.e. collection, storage, distribution, reception and dissemination points, it would at best be a slow and rather ponderous process, rather like early mainframe networks, and at worst like the M25 at 5.00p.m. on a Friday evening.

4.5 Robots and agents

Because networks can become traffic-bound, and because it is expensive to stay on-line, especially when searching for information, software – known as *search engines* or *net agents* – has been developed. These software 'robots' are being built with increasing intelligence to travel around the intranet – and even to cross over to the Internet – to search for information. Their beauty lies in the fact that the user need not be on-line while the search engine does its work. They can be redirected to 'kennels' where they will reside until needed. They can also be 'retrained' to make them more precise.

An example task for a search engine might be to search the on-line newspapers on the Internet and collect any pieces of information on a particular topic. The information collected will then be collated and presented as a complete résumé, ready for easy consumption.

Of course, it takes time and patience to configure the robots to get exactly what is required from the plethora of information available.

4.6 Making the right connections

For the busy manager the key to using networks successfully is to make sure that they make the right connections. This is easier said than done. The temptation is to 'get connected' to be open, receptive and easy to contact. This can lead to precious time being spent every day checking e-mail and listening to voice mail, much of which might be of only passing interest. This information overload will worsen. The speed and complexity of current technological development will require managers to learn to swim against the tide of information – or drown in it.

Visual telecommunications will spread as soon as PCs are delivered with a tiny camera built into the screen or the screen casing. When a phone call comes through, pictures of the caller and the recipient will appear on each other's screens. The camera will be switchable on and off so that anonymity can be protected if desired. At the same time, either party will be able to transmit on-screen material – a sales chart, for example – down the same line to be displayed on the other's computer. This form of visual communication will extend in due course to conference facilities, connecting a number of people via the visual communication network. The bandwidth required for this to work effectively will mean the use of optical fibre – this is already becoming widespread.

Intelligent data management will enable systems to sort and file data received and to encode and decode it automatically for transmission on to the network – thus avoiding all the current problems of trying to attach appropriately coded documents to e-mails and faxes. In addition, when information is broadcast the system (server and workstation) will decide if the user wants it and, if so, will file it at the appropriate location. This will be done by setting up a subject filing protocol for the system – or allowing the system to set up its own.

Access keys will be used to ensure that only certain people can get through. A caller who does not have an access key will be held on-line and the system will check whether they are to be put through. The same will apply to e-mail, faxes etc. This facility will allow the system to filter out junk communication whether oral or written. At the present time it is estimated that between 30 per cent and 60 per cent of communication is both unsolicited and unwanted, and this percentage will increase considerably.

Many other facilities will begin to appear on our networks: whether or not users are equipped to manage them effectively will depend on their knowledge and ability to make and use the new connections.

4.7 Internet developments

Two of the latest ideas, which will be used by both Internet and intranets, are *push technology* and *active desktops*. Both of these are particularly suited to intranets where users are on-line all the time. Push technology is akin to a TV signal broadcast to all sets that are switched on. The user identifies his area of interest and the relevant information is sent out automatically. There is no need to search or browse for it. This links particularly to active desktops, which either display or indicate that information has been received and is available for review; or open a window to interrupt current screen activity; or display a single, scrolling text line across the active screen.

If all these developments are taken together, the world of information provision is set to look very different. Events are moving very quickly. Link this to ideas such as continuous accounting and portable computer/communication devices and it can be seen that the world of information management, in terms of access to and presentation of information, is about to be transformed.

Legal developments

Imagine a situation in which a colleague sends you an e-mail which mentions a mutual acquaintance in unflattering terms. Is putting the message on the network a case of deliberate or wanton distribution of information that may damage their reputation? Many points such as this are not fully tested in the courts and there are likely to be some interesting legal battles in future. We are already beginning to see lawyers specialising in web matters.

Some concerns about being connected

Getting connected is now almost an imperative for many people in the West and in the tiger economies of the East. The Internet and the World Wide Web have revolutionised communications, information transfer and information search – so much is available to so many at a relatively low cost. With the arrival of intranets organisations can build their own equivalent of the Internet, with all the advantages this brings for efficient information management and communications. Of course, networks have to be carefully managed to be at their best and, with the arrival of new tools, they are becoming a boon to organisations and individuals alike.

The tendency for organisations to link their own intranets to the Internet begs the question of to what extent organisations want to open their doors to visitors from cyberspace. The security risks of linking to the Internet are considerable. Apart from allowing unwelcome access, there is also the prospect of picking up a virus in the process. Of course, viruses can be found and eliminated, and unwelcome visitors traced – by why run the risk of attracting them in the first place? Perhaps the main reason is the potential for using the international network for e-mail without the cost of installing an organisation-wide intranet to do the same thing. What has to be weighed up is whether this advantage is worth the security risk.

Telephony is a specialised technology, and building secure links across the telephone network is not easy. It is important to get the best possible advice not from those who stand to gain from your use of the system, i.e. service providers, but from independent advisers.

Then there is the prospect of staff spending time connected to the system, browsing for items that interest *them* – but which might not be concerned with work. They might import all sorts of data, games, software, etc., until their PC or the local servers are packed with unneeded and unwanted material.

In time, networks will provide all types of secure gates, with keys and passwords galore: until then it is worth taking great care to close the stable door before the horse bolts.

4.8 Summary

- Getting connected is primarily about becoming an Internet subscriber or becoming linked to the organisation's own intranet.
- Through being connected and 'browsing' a great deal of information can be gathered.
- Robots and net agents can be used to help with the collection of the information that is required.
- Traffic control can be an issue, and sometimes using the Internet can be a slow process.
- There are concerns about being connected, particularly in relation to security.

PART II
Information as a Commodity

Part of being informed is to be able to understand the nature and relevance of information as a commodity that is bought and sold. The theory underlying information is not particularly complex, and Part II provides a guide for managers to understanding the basics of information management.

Chapters 5 and 6 set out the basics of information theory and provide an introduction to some of the jargon so that the reader may put it into context. These two chapters provide an insight to the building blocks of information systems and offer a foundation for understanding.

Chapter 7 explores information as a resource and demonstrates how it can be stored and managed for use as and when required. Finally, Chapter 8 discusses the value of information, particularly in relation to its use in decision-making.

Part II offers some of the keys to understanding information and a basic approach to becoming an informed manager.

5 Information and Communication

5.1 Data capture

If the foundations of a building are not constructed properly the building, no matter how well designed, will collapse. The same is true of an information system. No matter how elegant the design of the system, if the basic needs for relevant, accurate, and timely data capture are not met then the system will fail.

Data is the outcome of specific transactions. If workers spend time on a particular job they record their hours against a job number. When they do this, data is created. This data may be used to calculate wages, to cost the job, as a basis for future estimating, and as a check on efficiency. So the same basic data may have many uses.

In data capture there are six critical questions to ask:

- What data do we have to capture?
- Why do we have to capture this data?
- Where can the data be captured?
- How can the data be captured?
- When can the data be captured?
- Who will capture the data?

There is a common belief, often fostered by ideas about modern technology, that the best approach is to trawl for information – to capture all data and then sort it afterwards. Computers, or so the argument goes, are big and fast enough to cope. In any case, isn't all data relevant? The answer is *no*. Data is all around us – our senses capture some, more passes by, but we are selective: we filter data and select on the basis of current relevance. In the modern business more data is captured than is – or ever can be – used. So why not collect only the data that is needed?

LIVERPOOL JOHN MOORES UNIVERSITY
LEARNING SERVICES

> ### The record of transport maintenance
>
> The transport manager had been trying for several years to get a detailed analysis of maintenance costs on his fleet of vehicles. With the help of the systems analyst he had devised a worksheet on which mechanics were to record their time and the materials used. Against each item they would insert a code indicating on which part of the vehicle the time/material was used. There were fifty codes in eight sections, all listed on the back of the worksheet. It seemed like a good idea and the transport manager had thought through the six questions on data capture.
>
> When the system was put into operation several things happened. First, jobs took longer because mechanics were spending time completing the detailed analysis. Second, the recording was not accurate, as mechanics either could not be bothered, or made mistakes. After several months of unusable, if not misleading, information the system was simplified. Time and materials were recorded against the eight main parts of the vehicle instead of against the fifty codes. The result was less detailed but more accurate, and gave relevant information which could be used.

Capturing data at source

There is an increasing move towards capturing data at source. A widely experienced example of this is the use of barcoding on grocery products, which is read by electronic point of sale (EPOS) machines. Another example would be the use of automated timing on production machines. Tachographs are used on commercial vehicles to keep a record of the time spent driving. Job accounting systems keep records of the work done on computers.

But not all primary data can be captured in this way. Much primary data has to be captured manually – either by being recorded on paper or input into some fixed or portable computer device. It is important to try to capture data at source in order to speed up the capture process and to avoid the risk of corruption to the data by subsequent handling.

Coding

Coding is used to help capture data in a meaningful way by providing a simplified way of describing the data and defining its use. So the barcode on a grocery product tells the system the item purchased. From this the price can be accessed at the till and a tally produced. In addition, the computer is able to produce information for stock ordering and sales analysis, and profit statements for the store – all from the simple barcode.

Codes can also be added to data after capture to specify where the data is to be stored, i.e. as a form of address (this is what a nominal ledger code does). Again this can be done automatically as part of the processing cycle, or manually.

?

> ### 5.1 Data generation
>
> Consider for a moment your own job. Think about the data that you generate from the transactions that you are engaged in. Then consider how much of this is captured and what it is used for. Then think about how you could minimise the data captured to only that which is of use to you, or someone else.

5.2 Data storage

The key to data storage (and the word *key* is both important and appropriate) is the extent to which access to the data is required. The concept of access incorporates a number of requirements, principal among which are:

- frequency of access;
- access paths;
- access authority; and
- access restrictions.

When these requirements have been considered the most appropriate form and location of data storage can be determined.

Frequency of access

If data is to be accessed every few minutes it needs to be stored in a different way from data which is to be accessed only once a year. So in considering the storage of data the frequency of access must be established. There might be five categories: frequent, regular, routine, infrequent, and rarely.

Access paths

If data is to be accessed by only one person it can probably be located with that person. If everybody in the company needs to access it, e.g. in the case of product data, then it will need to be held on a suitable database and located where it can be reached by everybody. So there could be five categories of path: individual, department, division, company, and group.

Access authority

If only certain people have access to data because of its sensitivity, e.g. in the case of product price files, then it will need to be stored in a software- or hardware-protected environment. Five suitable categories might be: open, restricted, confidential, secret, and closed.

Access restrictions

When data is accessed, the way it can be used could be restricted – for example, when it can only be read it is filed in read-only memory (ROM), or when it can be added to but not changed, or changed but not deleted. This depends upon who has access: for example, product price files can be accessed by sales staff, but changed only by the sales manager. Five suitable categories might be: no restriction, delete, amend, update (add to), and read only.

If these four requirements and the various categories are considered, a data storage matrix can be constructed. This provides a simple, but not exhaustive, way of looking at the most appropriate approach to storage.

Figure 5.1: Data-storage matrix

Requirements			Categories		
Frequency	Frequent	Regular	Routine	Infrequent	Rarely
Paths	Individual	Department	Division	Company	Group
Authority	Open	Restricted	Confidential	Secret	Closed
Restrictions	None	Delete	Amend	Update	Read-only

By using this simple matrix it is possible to identify over 90 per cent of data storage requirements and to define what is appropriate in terms of hardware and software for each possibility. For example:

▪ Frequency – *Regular*;
▪ Path – *Department*;
▪ Authority – *Restricted*; and
▪ Restrictions – *Amend*.

This data could be held on a local-area network (LAN) serving the department concerned, where passwords and authority codes are used.

? | **5.2 Your data needs**

What different storage needs do you have for the data that is essential to your own work? Use the matrix to help you to define the range of different storage needs you might have.

Computers as data stores

To store data on computers an indication is needed of where the data is to go and how it is to be retrieved. To understand the way that the computer copes with filing and retrieving data it is useful to examine the language that is used. There are six main words for which a definition is needed.

▪ *File*. An organised and structured collection of data so as to facilitate the necessary access.
▪ *Directory*. A collection of files.

- *Index.* A series of identifiers of files or of data held on files.
- *Key* or *keyword.* A group of characters used in the identification of an item and to facilitate access to it.
- *Location.* A storage position that can hold one computer word.
- *Address.* A number which identifies a location within the computer's memory.

The location and address are allocated automatically by the computer. So, to file data in the computer, each item must be given an identifier or *key*. This item is held in a *file* to which a name is given. This file is in a *directory* which is also named, and for which an *index* may be created. This structure enables data to be put into the file and accessed later. Links can also be provided between data items in different files, creating a large and complex system of data storage. This is covered in more detail in a later section.

5.3 Reporting

Data is not necessarily stored in the sequence in which it provides useful information; in fact this is rarely the case. For data to be produced in a usable form it usually has to be related to, merged with, collated, aggregated, and presented so the user can make use of it.

Four levels at which data is manipulated to produce meaningful information are as follows.

- *Transactional.* Data which emanates from the primary transactions of the business, e.g. each sale, purchase, delivery, etc., is usually accumulated in transaction-related groupings. These groupings are most useful and are reported (displayed/printed) as an initial control of business activity, e.g. sales per product per customer. The data is then aggregated to provide information at the next level. It is probable, and in certain situations essential, that files of original transaction data will be retained for reference and audit requirements.
- *Operational.* Operational data is usually concerned with what the business is doing on a day-to-day basis. This might be a record of how or where the material issued from store is used. Other examples would be the tonnes produced per shift, or quotations issued in the day etc.

  Operational data is reported to provide statistics of what is happening. This might then be compared to what it was expected or planned would be happening, to produce information about the operations of the business.
- *Managerial.* Information that is used for management of the business is a combination of transactional and operational data reported in meaningful combinations and relationships. This is the level of reporting to which most attention is paid in most information systems. However, if the reporting and control of data at the transactional and operational levels is not of the highest standards, then management information must also be suspect.

  In the scenario at the beginning of this chapter the transactional data of material issues and time recording per man were accurate. However, the operational data of the work done on each vehicle was not. The result was that the managerial reports were not usable – in fact they were misleading.

The marketing report

The marketing manager had requested a report of the weekly sales of two products, Tinto and Pinko, from each branch over a ten-week period. He wanted the sales quantities, average prices, and sales trends for each branch over the ten weeks, and a comparison between branches.

To produce this report, data of quantity and price had to be extracted from the transaction data (which was accumulated and stored for each week for each product for each branch). Once this data had been accessed, and a file created to store it, it was possible to write a report-generating program to produce the report.

The information for sales trends, and comparison between branches, was presented graphically. The marketing manager could request the data for each branch and then create the graphs on screen. In this way he was able to manipulate the information in any combination he thought might be useful. When he had found what he wanted he was able to print the information. It was also possible to create a file of the information, and to store the report-generating program for future use.

- *Planning.* Data in the planning level is not generated from the routine business process as are transactional and operational data. It is instead generated by a management process of forecasting ahead and deciding on what the business is aiming or expecting to do in the future. It may be based on the data from the transactional and operational levels, but is more likely to be based on other factors, such as market intelligence and economic predictors. It is created to influence decision-making and to provide a 'barometer'.

In the scenario above the marketing manager might have wanted to introduce planning data of expected average prices and sales levels. To do this it would have meant that data for these planned levels would have to be input into the system to be available for later reporting.

Flexible reporting

The modern information system provides managers with considerable flexibility in what can be reported from the four basic levels described. This flexibility means that there is scope for accessing information in different ways at different times to cope with changing needs.

It is probable that certain routine and regular information will be required in the same format. Files that facilitate this can be produced automatically at the appropriate intervals. It is also probable that managers will become accustomed to seeing information presented in a certain way and want to maintain this format unchanged for long periods.

Presenting information

The following list shows the principles of presentation, which are all to do with the relevance of the information presented.

▪ Provide the minimum information possible.
▪ Concentrate on the most significant information.
▪ Report the interesting exceptions.
▪ Indicate the degree of tolerance, e.g. ±5 per cent.
▪ Use graphs and charts to compare, or show mix.
▪ Use graphics only when they add impact and meaning.
▪ Trends and possibilities are more meaningful than history, although they may be based on it.
▪ Change focus from time to time, and use a zoom perception to home in on detail as well as looking at the wide angle.

Reporting media

The medium used should neither enhance nor detract from the meaningfulness of the information it presents. The two most commonly used media are paper and the computer screen, and both have their advantages and disadvantages. With modern desktop publishing, paper-based reporting of information has taken on a new lease of life. Where paper wins for portability and convenience, the computer screen wins for flexibility of manipulation and adaptability.

Informal information

Not all the information that a manager uses for decision-making is based on data collected from the transactions of the business. There are other sources of 'informal' information picked up from the manager's own experience, the comments of colleagues, the press, magazines and so on. All these informal sources of information can influence the manager. The role of 'formal' information from the data collected in the business has to be put into the wider context of the total environment in which the manager operates. Relying only on information collected internally is comparable to driving a car by looking only at the instruments on the dashboard, rather than looking out of the windows at the environment – a rather hazardous thing to do.

?

5.3 The credit control report
Imagine that you are responsible for managing the outstanding debtors for your organisation. If you do not grant credit try to imagine being in a situation where managing outstanding debt is important.
Referring to the principles of presenting information, what information would you want, and how often would you want it, to control debtors effectively?

5.4 Communications

People sometimes say that the purpose of information systems is to communicate. This is not so. People, not systems, communicate. Systems do transfer data from one location to another, often over considerable distances, and they do this very fast, but this is *data transfer*. Communication takes place only when a message is transmitted and its *meaning* interpreted.

Of course, this broad idea of communication can be used to describe the many and varied ways in which messages can be constructed, transmitted and received. In the technology age, the term 'communication' has become more or less synonymous with the *mechanisms* of communication rather than with the *process* itself.

Communication is a process that includes the formulation, transmission, reception, and interpretation of information. This process takes place when a diner in a restaurant orders a meal, or when a fax is sent to the other side of the world. In both cases, the basic process is the same.

Communication mechanisms, media, or methods, are the means by which the communication process is carried out. In the case of the restaurant it is the use of the voice for transmission, and the ear for reception. In the case of the fax it is a message from one facsimile machine via a telecommunication network to another facsimile machine. The mechanisms are different, but the process is the same.

Production problems

When working in a quarrying company, TJ came across the same communication situation in three different divisions being handled in completely different ways. The situation was concerned with how the divisional production manager became aware of production problems at the various quarries under his management.

In Division A, the production manager spent most of his time visiting his quarries and seeing for himself what was going on. Every evening he phoned his production clerk and asked where he should visit the next day. The production clerk was informed by the quarries of any difficulties. If there was an emergency the production clerk could contact the production manager because he always knew where the manager was.

In Division B, the production manager worked from his central office and phoned each of his quarry managers every day. In the discussion he was able to establish conditions. If he went to visit a quarry he could still make his calls. He believed in trusting his managers to get on and do their jobs, and to tell him when they were having problems.

In Division C, the production manager received a daily report from each quarry which he studied each morning. He could then contact the quarry or make a visit if he thought it necessary.

These three different approaches suited the individuals involved and each seemed as effective as the others. Yet each of the managers thought his colleagues did it in the wrong way.

?

> ## 5.4 Ways to communicate
>
> Think of one area of communication that you undertake regularly. Now write down as many ways as possible that you could do it. Remember the process is the same: you must think of as many different methods you can can. Ignore whether what you say is obvious or 'science fiction': you may stumble on an even better way than your present one!

5.5 Noise and media

Perhaps the greatest single problem in communication, no matter which medium is chosen, is noise. Imagine a telephone call when the line is noisy with hisses and crackles, or attempting to talk to somebody at a noisy party. The background noise interferes with the communication process. The message constructed and sent out may be OK, but what is received could be distorted by noise. A well-known story from the first world war concerns a message sent out from the front: 'Send reinforcements, we are going to advance'. Noise caused the message to be received: 'Send three-and-fourpence, we're going to a dance'!

Noise can be of three main types.

- *Environmental.* Environmental noise is interference from outside the communication process and media which interferes with the communication process. It might be the noise of a busy office, or a passing aircraft, or the sound from a busy street. It interferes with the process and so there is a danger that the message is not heard, heard differently than intended, or understood differently. The important thing is to check with the recipient what they have heard and understood, or to delay the communication until the noise has subsided.

- *Physical.* Most of the media available for carrying communications can distort the message because of physical noise emanating from the equipment itself. As telecommunication systems improve, this is becoming less of a problem. However, electronic mail messages have been known to arrive at the wrong address, and fax messages occasionally look like barcodes instead of readable text.

- *Intellectual.* Intellectual noise is far greater a problem than the other two types of noise. This is the noise that communicators insert into their own messages. It is done either accidentally or deliberately. The effect is the same: the message is blurred.

  Intellectual noise comes from the communicator's lack of clarity, or from a deliberate attempt to disguise the real message.

  Here are two examples of intellectually noisy messages.

  'Having taken due regard of our responsibilities to our shareholders and our need to appear to be making a serious attempt to deal with current economic problems it seems likely that we will have to lose some of our people.'

The *real* message is:

'*In order to reduce costs we will have to sack people.*'

Here is another one.

'*I have been studying the latest figures for the fabric division and I note that we are running behind planned sales by a considerable margin. I would like to talk to you about this at some convenient moment, and perhaps you could give the matter some thought and contact me to arrange a meeting when you are ready.*'

The *real* message is:

'*I want you to come to see me immediately to tell me what has happened to fabric sales. The figures are terrible.*'

5.5 Intellectual noise

Consider the following passage.

'*I have been intending to talk to you for quite some time, and the moment never seems quite right. Perhaps you could let me know when it would be appropriate for us to meet.*

'*I should perhaps also say that I have a number of concerns about the way that you have been interpreting some of the policy circulars and I would like to discuss your approach to how we might improve this situation in the future. You will probably think I am making a mountain out of a molehill, but molehills have a way of becoming extremely frustrating even though they are small. Give me a call to arrange a convenient time for us to meet.*'

Have a go at interpreting this one and write your version in the space below.

?

> ### 5.6 The order form
>
> Here is a communication problem for you to solve.
>
> Orders are taken in the central order office for twelve production units in the local district. Customers phone in the afternoon for deliveries to be made the next day. The order office take the orders, decide which is the most appropriate unit to deliver and then phone the orders through to the units at 5.00pm so they can be made ready for delivery the next day.
>
> Many errors occur in addresses, quantities and products, and a lot of additional work has to be done to mollify customers and to correct the mistakes.
>
> How would you deal with this?

5.6 Knowledge and learning

The real value of information lies in the way it impacts on our current store of knowledge and whether it aids our learning. The meaning, and hence value, of information will vary from one person to another. So the same piece of information can have different meanings and values. Here is a quotation by Duryer.

> 'Like management itself, management information has vital human implications.... To demonstrate a point, then, let's consider the implications to various people of a train whistle penetrating the evening dusk.
>
> 'To the saboteur crouching in a culvert it might signify the failure of his mission because the whistle indicates that the train has already passed his detonating charge without causing an explosion. To the lonely wife it means the return of her travelling husband. To the man with his foot caught in the switch down the track it foreshadows doom.... For another (preparing for bed) it signifies time for prayer.... In brief, the nature and significance of any information are fundamentally and primarily functions of the attitudes, situations and relevant responsibilities with respect thereto of the people involved with it....
>
> '... Information is management information only to the extent to which the manager needs or wants it; and it is significant to him only in terms of its relation to his accumulation of relevant knowledge and plans and to his personal responsibility.'

It seems fair to say that information has value only in as far as it increases the knowledge of recipients which in turn extends their learning so that some changes in behaviour are effected. In other words information has value in relation to its use.

Knowledge

It is important to divide thinking about knowledge into two elements: a store of data, and understanding.

Incredible amounts of information can be stored in the human brain. Much of this data falls into the category of facts, i.e. things that are known, such as telephone numbers, addresses, names, etc. These facts are unrelated – they are just facts. They could be unloaded into suitable external files such as address books, diaries, and so on. People do, in fact, clutter their brains with these facts and it takes practice to sort out and remove the clutter.

Understanding is different. It might make use of facts, but it is a deeper knowledge of what the facts received might mean. Understanding helps people to interpret and sort incoming information. Understanding is gained from experience, and is likewise limited by experience.

Learning

Learning takes place when knowledge which has been gathered is used in a way that extends the individual's experience of his environment. The degree of learning is tested by response to events, and it is this view of learning which is so important in the information management arena.

People learn differently. Kolb defined four primary learning styles:

- concrete experience (feeling);
- reflective observation (watching);
- abstract conceptualisation (thinking); and
- active experimentation (doing).

From these four positions, Kolb developed four main learning approaches:

- converging (thinking then doing);
- assimilating (listening then doing);
- accommodating (feeling then doing); and
- diverging (feeling then watching).

Of course, these four are only the broad learning styles. People can learn from a variety of these approaches.

In this context, then, information plays a vital role which will vary considerably from person to person. This is one of the reasons why managers use information so differently.

Figure 5.2: Kolb's learning approaches

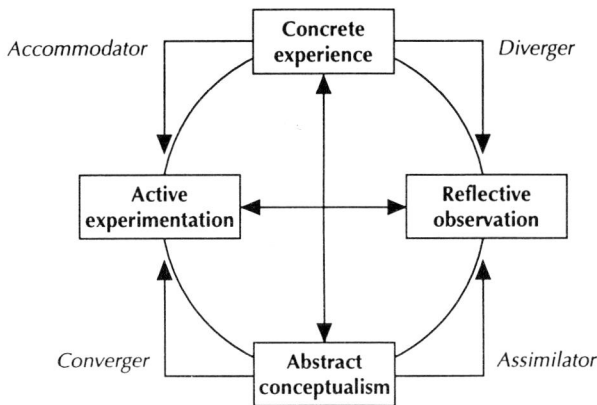

<table>
<tr><td></td><td>Concrete experience</td><td></td></tr>
</table>

Accommodator — Concrete experience — Diverger

Active experimentation — Reflective observation

Converger — Abstract conceptualism — Assimilator

Transport utilisation

TJ carried out a study for a quarrying company on the efficiency with which vehicles were being used. The information he wanted to gather to establish efficiency was: earnings per tonne/mile, and earnings per vehicle hour. Neither piece of information was currently available from the existing system. TJ spent some time laboriously collating this information manually for a period of three months and, at the end of the period, presented the information to a meeting of transport managers for their comments.

At the meeting he asked them to think about how they could increase earnings per tonne/mile, and then how they could increase earnings per vehicle hour. The outcome was a completely new approach to how the vehicle fleet was managed and distribution organised.

Using information

In the scenario above, TJ did several things. First he put forward his interpretation of efficiency of vehicle utilisation. Second, he presented some new information to people with long experience in the area of transport management. They were able very quickly to relate this new information to their existing experience, i.e. to understand it. Then he was able to work through how this new understanding could be used to increase their learning about managing the efficiency of the vehicles. Finally the new information supported changes in the way things were done.

5.7 Quality of information

?

> ### 5.7 Quality of information
>
> How would you define high-quality information?

In later sections of this text, various methods are suggested in which a value can be placed on information. But finding information useful and of value does not necessarily indicate that the information is of high quality. To have quality, information needs to be *relevant, reliable* and *robust*.

Relevant information

Information is relevant when the recipient is able to use it to perform more effectively than would be possible without it. This might be information that is produced regularly or information which is requested to deal with a particular need. How important the information is will depend to what extent it impacts on the activity of the recipient.

Reliable information

Reliable information is *timely*, so that it is available when it is needed; *accurate*, to the extent necessary for the way it is to be used; and *verifiable* by analysis of the supporting data.

> ## Disappearing profits
>
> The road-surfacing division of a large construction group was watching the profits built into its contracts disappearing as contracts approached completion. Analysis of the costing information showed that the main causes were:
>
> (a) material usage; and
> (b) direct labour.
>
> After a review of procedures it was decided to introduce a new system based on daily measurements of materials used and hours worked in relation to the work completed that day. This was done in physical terms, i.e. tonnes, and hours per square metre laid. These performance indicators were compared with the standards built into contract prices and immediate action taken to rectify any variation. The use of this timely and more relevant information stopped the erosion of profits, which was clearly verified from subsequent management accounts.

Robust information

Information is robust when it can stand up to the rigours of time, human frailty, system failure and organisational changes.

Time is a good test, since most information rapidly becomes obsolete. So if information is to cope it has to be able to move with the times.

Human frailty will affect information by causing mistakes in data handling, coding, etc. Controls and checks must exist to identify and correct such errors so that the information is not corrupted.

System failure can damage information and so it must be protected from the effects of failure, both in terms of content and timeliness.

Organisational changes may inflict lasting damage on information unless the structure of the files, methods of access and reporting are protected from such changes.

Credit control information

'When supplying the construction industry, credit control can be a very important element in protecting the size and quality of profit. To do this we need high-quality information.' This was the statement made to TJ by the financial director of the company he was advising. After he had studied what was needed he recommended a system with the following attributes.

- A computer-based, open-item sales ledger, updated daily with invoices and cheques/cash received.
- The system was accessible by customer number or name, with special accesses available for large and late debtors.
- When a customer was accessed, the first screen gave a summary of outstanding aged debt. By selecting any month a screen of the detailed outstanding invoices for that month were shown. Invoices in dispute were highlighted.
- The system was used for cash/cheque allocation, chasing outstanding money, and management information.
- At the end of every day the outstanding position of the data was copied (backed up), together with a copy of that day's transactions.
- Particular customer records could be downloaded to PCs for investigation/reconciliation. Access was restricted and controls of all system changes existed.

There were a variety of other checks and, from time to time, the work of staff was verified by supervisors. After a long period of use and with several changes of computer it is still functioning well and providing high-quality information.

5.8 Summary

- Data capture and storage is a critical element of good-quality information, but it is only part of the overall picture.
- Reporting of information is done at a variety of levels: transactional, operational, management and planning.
- Communication is about transmitting, receiving and understanding messages and not about data transfer.
- Communication can be interrupted by noise from the environment, the system, and through people introducing their own 'noisy language'.
- Use of information is dependent, to some extent, on the way people learn. Kolb identified four learning styles: converging; assimilating; accommodating; diverging.
- Good-quality information is relevant, reliable and robust.

6 Information Theory

6.1 Systems theory

The word *system* is used in many different ways, and mostly in some specific context which provides a definition – for example, the solar system is taken to mean the system of planets and associated satellites which move in orbit round the sun. Each component of the system moves in some relationship to the other components.

Here is a definition of a system.

> 'A system comprises a number of elements which are connected or related, and which are organised, either naturally or by design, to achieve some purpose.'

A system must have a purpose and it functions with the achievement of that purpose as its overriding control mechanism. To achieve the purpose the system will feed off and manipulate the resources available to it. The system receives inputs, works upon them, and converts or transforms them into outputs which meet the objectives of the system. This process is not carried out in isolation but within an environment alongside or linked to other systems.

A purchasing system in a company is a typical example. The system is linked to a number of other systems, including the supplier's sales-order processing system, the stores control system, the accounting system, and the quality control system.

Each separate purchase is a transaction which flows through the system and this process is continuous. Systems of this kind are referred to as *open systems* because they interact with other systems around them, information flowing in and out at various points in the system.

Closed systems, where there is no interaction with the environment or other systems, are rare, especially in the business environment. A closed system will have no input and output points and would not react to control information from outside. The water heater in a cistern is an example. The thermostat is set at a certain temperature and will operate when the water falls below that temperature, and switch off when it again reaches the required temperature. There is no external input or output, although a clock may be included in the control cycle.

Systems hierarchy

An individual business is an open system which is also a subsystem of an industry, which is itself a subsystem of the economy of the country, which is part of the world economy.

The enterprise is constructed of a hierarchy of subsystems which fit together rather like a jigsaw.

Figure 6.1: Hierarchy of subsystems

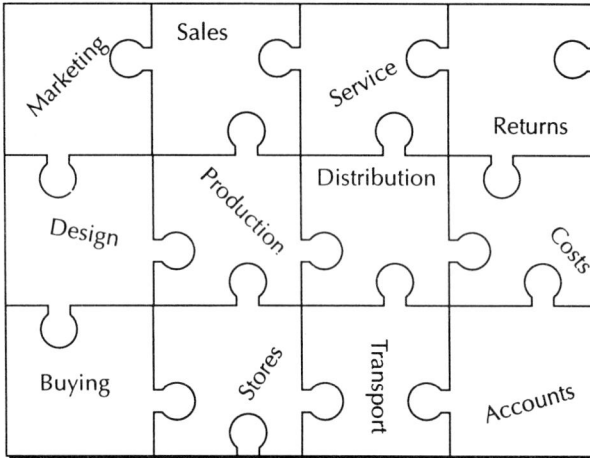

The particular systems structure of a business is very important to the design of good systems. The most effective systems infrastructure places an emphasis on those subsystems which have the greatest impact on the achievement of business objectives.

> **?**
>
> ### 6.1 A systems infrastructure I know
>
> Think about the environment in which you work, and see if you can plot the systems infrastructure. When you have done this select the systems which you think should be given emphasis in order to optimise the organisation's performance.

The nature of systems

Individual systems have a nature of their own.

- *Deterministic systems* are those which act in a definite way, devoid of uncertainty. If a certain signal is received by the system, then it can be predicted exactly what the system will do (assuming it works in accordance with its basic rules). The example of the water heater is a deterministic system.
- *Probabilistic systems* are those in which the outcome is uncertain, where

predictions can be made only with the qualification that they are likely outcomes or reactions.

- *Adaptive systems* are those which can be adapted to suit the environment when changes take place. Information systems should be adaptive, but unfortunately many are rigid.
- *Rigid systems* are those which do not adapt to change and are therefore of limited value. However, some circumstances call for such rigidity – e.g. a system for handling dangerous materials, or maintenance procedures on aircraft: here, the discipline of a rigid system is of particular value. However, both natural and man-made systems must adapt if they are to survive.

Entropy

Entropy, or spontaneous change, occurs in both natural and man-made systems. This might be hard to imagine for a computer system operating in a programmed and controlled environment, but it does happen. And very often it happens in a random fashion.

In closed systems, entropy operates by the gradual reduction in the system's capability to perform. Take the water heater example: through time the system will become less effective. Minor changes in the electrical circuits will affect the timing, and so on.

In open systems, new forms of input will cause the system to try to cope, adapt and deal with the difference. Take the example of a building society system for handling customer payments and receipts. In a training exercise before the system 'went live' staff attempted to withdraw more from an account than its balance. The system allowed this and printed the balance as zero – it had been programmed not to show a minus balance. Of course, this was changed to prevent this type of transaction.

Expert systems

Expert systems are systems built to use a set of rules to manipulate information (its knowledge base) to arrive at conclusions based on inferences generated by the rules. The set of rules is referred to as an *inference engine*. This rule set is built by experts in the particular subject area.

An example might be a diagnostic system for establishing the causes of mechanical failure in a jet engine.

The symptoms of the failure are input and, using its knowledge base and inference engine, the system is able to suggest probable causes. It can also generate questions to obtain more information so that it can make its suggestions more specific.

Expert systems are sometimes referred to as *intelligent systems*, which they are *not*. They depend completely on the human intelligence of their builders, and replicate any weakness in this intelligence.

Neural systems

Although the kind of expert system described above is useful, there is now the potential to build systems that learn by using neural networks. These are built to replicate the functioning of the human brain, albeit a tiny replica – a few tens of neurons compared to the billions of neurons in the brain.

The way the computer works with bits of memory switched on or off is the same as the way in which the brain works, with individual neurons charged or not charged with an electric current. The brain, it is believed, works by linking neurons by means of synapses. When two neurons are charged simultaneously their synapse connection is reinforced and is recognised as a meaningful value. A combination of such connections is recognised as a pattern. Additional connections are made to record new, i.e. unrecognised, patterns and so the brain learns.

In theory, if a group of microprocessors (representing neurons) were to be connected by circuits that operate randomly (synapses) a model of the brain could be built. This is not viable at the present time, but such networks can be simulated on the computer, and these are used to recognise patterns.

However, the practical application of neural networks is still limited by the power and scope of computers. Even a simple commercial application would need thirty or forty neurons linked by thousands of connections. Each of these connections needs its own behaviour pattern to be represented mathematically and to be calculated when data is input. Although modern computers are very fast, they cannot cope with anything more than very small simulations, at least not at a commercially viable cost.

Requisite variety

To be really effective, an information infrastructure must be able to cope with a wide variety of operational uses and demands. If this variety can be predicted, or if the possibilities are recognised, then the infrastructure can be built to accommodate the variety.

With the advent of database systems it is important that the changes made through data degradation and redundancy does not reduce the ability to access data at a variety of levels. For example, if customers who have ceased to trade with the company, or who have ceased to trade themselves, are removed from the active database they should be transferred to a separate 'closed file' and an indication left on the database of where the data can be found. In a similar way, individual transactions which have been aggregated on the database should also be held in some form in the original transaction detail. One of the problems with creating corporate databases managed via data dictionaries is enabling access to the data for the range or variety of uses for which the data might be needed.

> ### Systems that train as they work
>
> The new computer system was to provide facilities for a wide range of tasks to support international banking needs. Only the most experienced experts could fully understand what was needed in every commercial situation. For the system to function effectively there were two options:
>
> (a) train people to a high standard in international banking; or
> (b) employ only experts to use the system.
>
> Neither alternative was feasible in a fast-moving competitive market.
>
> The answer was to build the system so that people could train as they worked. This was done by including three additional elements into the system, with the help of an international banking expert. The first was a comprehensive context-sensitive help function, which would work on three levels: simple prompts, advice on what to do, or complete transaction guidance.
>
> The second feature would be a training support function to provide simple examples and simulations of the commercial situation for operators to learn from. This would enable them to deal with the current task and to learn and gain confidence for the future.
>
> The third element was a feature to monitor the work of the individual to see the extent to which they were learning and developing skill in using the system.
>
> Once the knowledge base was complete it would support any request concerned with international banking. As changes took place the knowledge base was extended.

The scenario above indicates how requisite variety can be provided for if the need is acknowledged from the beginning. The system as described is used by experts and relative newcomers to provide a very effective service to customers.

6.2 The changing state of information

'It is quite possible for management to collect more information than it can use to advantage, or which is more costly, or hinders production more, than the information is worth. This is a real danger that has to be guarded against continuously, for routine that serves a valuable purpose when initiated may cease to be useful by some later change in conditions.'

The quote above is from *Factory Administration and Accounts* by E T Elbourne (The Library Press, 1914).

Information can have a life cycle of any length. It can arise, be used and discarded in a few seconds, or it can be a constant source of reference and value.

Most managers will have experienced the feeling that the information they are giving to management is not exactly what is required. But trying to find out what *is* wanted can be a frustrating task.

Just tell me what you want

The meeting was about an hour old. TJ had asked the management team about the availability of information. They had each taken some time to think about the information that they *had* to have to function effectively. Then he asked them to indicate how much of this information they received. The responses were varied, but most people received only a portion of what they believed they needed.

The management accountant was getting very agitated.

'But I keep telling you that if I know what you want I can probably organise the system to produce it.'

'Yes, but it keeps changing. What I need now is not what I needed last week,' said the production manager. 'Last week the problem was the delay in production on Fret gears; this week I'm concerned about the cost of the work we're planning to subcontract to Webbs.'

TJ then suggested that the team should try to decide what information was useful to them on a regular basis and what kinds of information they needed access to as and when the need arose.

TJ suggested to the management accountant that the regular information could become the focus of his 'company information system', and that the other information could become the focus of individual 'personal information systems' for each manager.

Personalised information systems

To build a personalised information system, the decisions taken by managers, the information they decide they need, the source of the information and a means of accessing that source must all be identified. Such a personalised system can be built and maintained on a PC and changed as necessary to reflect the manager's changing needs. Instead of waiting for reports, managers can access the information they need, when they need it. They can also take some responsibility for the maintenance of their own systems in a currently useful state.

6.3 Information economics

> ## Assessing information costs
>
> TJ was determined to change the monthly reporting system which generated a 50-page book for each of the six divisions and a group book of 30 pages. To put his case across he calculated the cost of producing each of the documents and for the next board meeting affixed a price on each book.
>
> The response was what he hoped for: a demand to investigate the minimum information necessary to run the business with the focus on its key result areas. The outcome for the business was a new information infrastructure that was more effective and much less costly than the old system.

Of course, *value* and *cost* are relative terms. They can sometimes be calculated and related, but even then the answer does not necessarily provide a clear guide to the underlying economics of information.

The value of information

Perhaps the first point to make is that the value of information varies depending upon who receives it, when they receive it, and whether they can make use of it. But placing a financial, as well as a utility, value on it is another matter.

The vast expenditure on information system development implies that information is valuable. Some of this is in search of the competitive edge, some in search of improvements in business operations, and some in search of new opportunities, and the avoidance of threats. But how is the value of this investment justified? Here are a few ideas of information economics.

It's what I don't know that worries me

Reducing the risk in virtually any business decision is a fundamental factor in information economics. But this is where the basic economic law of diminishing returns comes into play. See Figure 6.2.

Figure 6.2: Law of diminishing returns

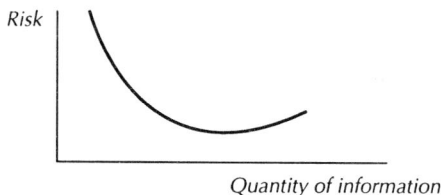

Quantity of information

As more information is available so risk lessens, but then a point is reached where more information begins to blur the issue and risk increases. However, as Peter Drucker says in his book *The Practice of Management*:

> 'The manager will never be able to get all the facts he should have. Most decisions have to be based on incomplete knowledge – either because the information is not available or it would cost too much in time and money to get it. To make sound decisions it is not necessary to have all the facts; but it is necessary to know what information is lacking in order to judge how much of a risk the decision involves, as well as the degree of precision and rigidity that the proposed course of action can afford. For there is nothing more treacherous – or alas, more common – than the attempt to make precise decisions on the basis of coarse and incomplete information.'

The reduction of risk can have a value which can be expressed in financial terms. If, for example, the loss from failure of a particular project is £10,000, then we can quickly estimate how much we are willing to spend on information to help to ensure it succeeds. If the cost of failure were to be the business's existence then we would probably spend as much as we could to avoid this occurrence.

The law of escalating demand

As information becomes more readily available more is demanded. This is one of the reasons for the massive increase in the investment in information systems, and for the transfer of much of the workforce from making things to processing information about other people making things (mainly in so-called third-world countries).

This is apparent in any business. Managers ask for additional information about price trends. When they get it, they ask for comparisons with different periods and products. When they get that, they ask for a comparison with market trends, and so on. Often these requests become enshrined in regular reporting procedures.

The law of praxis

Praxis is habitual and accustomed practice, and applies to information which is used in a habitual way. Its analysis and interpretation takes place in accordance with established organisational practice. These established rules are not challenged: they are the very bedrock of the organisation's mechanisms of control. To change them would be to risk the collapse of established order. So month after month, year after year, information is presented and interpreted in the same dogmatic, and often inappropriate, ways.

For example, there are organisations that still compare results for one period with those for the same period in the previous year, as if the two were related. There are organisations that compare results for one period against a budget for that period set, say, nine months previously. Not that these comparisons might not be useful, but they are made out of habit rather than out of some consideration for what is relevant to the moment.

The law of necessity

The luxuries we demand today become tomorrow's necessities.

> ## *If only I could know...*
>
> The chief executive was speaking on the telephone: this is his side of the conversation.
>
> 'The problem at the moment is that I don't have the information I need about the new development.'
> 'You could be right, but I simply don't know.'
> 'I suppose that market research might help, but it's so expensive.'
> 'It won't do any harm to talk to them, I suppose. I'll give them a call, thanks for your help, cheerio.'
>
> A short time later he interviewed and hired a firm of market researchers. The information they provided after a study enabled the chief executive to be more confident about the new development, which subsequently turned out to be a success. The company now has its own market research department employing four highly paid people.

It seems that the basic economics of consumerism are flourishing in the world of information. Yet for all the information available and all the billions of pounds spent on it, companies still go bust. A recession is still as damaging as it ever was, and the competitive edge is still as illusory for most businesses as it ever was.

The lack of information

The cost of providing information can be, and often is, evaluated in the business accounts, but what is often missing in such cost information is the implication of the 'lack of information'. This can create a significant 'non-financial' – in the sense of 'non-accountable' – cost to the business.

Imagine a builders' merchant where, on a regular basis, customers found that the supplies they required were out of stock. The storeman would apologise and the customer would go elsewhere. No record was kept of this 'lost sale'. This in turn meant that the benefits of increasing stockholding levels could not be reliably evaluated, and levels were kept low to keep stockholding costs down. When a study was carried out to assess 'lost sales' stocks of a wide range of products were increased between 20 and 30 per cent.

6.4 Relevance and redundancy of information

Windows of opportunity

There comes a moment – a 'window of opportunity' – when managers have a chance to use information effectively. These windows of opportunity are loosely known as decisions. When a decision has to be made, managers have to weigh up the information they have and make a choice of which course of action to take.
These windows of opportunity can be divided into three levels.

- *Mechanical decisions* are highly structured with easy access to the data required. many of these decisions can be automated, and are a feature of closed systems.
- *Routine decisions* are made less frequently, but are still structured and with a known data requirement. These decisions are typical of most operational systems and, although not automated, are relatively straightforward.
- *Complex decisions* are made infrequently, are unstructured, and depend largely on current circumstances, often with an unknown data requirement. These are the decisions that most senior managers are involved with, and many relate directly to people.

Moments of decision

Looking a little more closely at these three windows of opportunity to use information, it can be seen that the information is required exactly at the moment of decision. When this is, and how long it lasts, changes at each level.

Mechanical decisions

In a mechanical decision, information is used automatically as part of a formalised process. The decision has been made before on many occasions, and so the rules for the decision have become well established.

Each item of information received has a direct impact upon the decision, according to the predetermined rules. This form of decision is found in many different areas. One of these is automated process control. Materials flow along a production line, gauges and electrodes are used to measure sizes, temperature, consistency, etc. As each measurement is made, it is compared automatically with the required standard. If there is any variation, the production process is automatically adjusted to correct it. The measurements are continuous so that the production process operates at a high level of quality.

Similar decisions occur in administrative procedures. Payroll is a good example. The decision of how much tax and social security to deduct from an employee's cheque is a mechanical one relating to hours, the employee's pay, tax to date and tax code. With the information on hand, the calculations are automatic.

Mechanical decisions use information in a highly structured way. Only specific predetermined items of information are required. All other information is ignored. The system recognises this and is designed to feed the decision with only the information it needs. From time to time the decision rules change, and when this happens the information flows need to be adjusted.

It is in this area of mechanical decisions that the computer reigns supreme. As long as the decision rules have been correctly programmed and the information flows are accurate, the computer's speed and reliability ensures that the decisions are made as required. Of course, it must be remembered that it is humans who set the standards and rules in the first place – the machine only acts on them.

Routine decisions

When it is known that a routine decision is to be made, the exact rules are not known and so it is possible to only partially predict what information will be required. This means that some form of initiative has to be taken at the decision window to select information that is relevant, at the time the decision is made. Routine decisions have to be made regularly, but each time the decision is made the environment will have changed, and so information does not have an immediate and predicted effect on the decision.

Imagine the daily route plan for a delivery driver. The decision about the planned route will depend on the orders to be delivered, the addresses, the distances, current state of the roads, and estimated driving times. Each day the decision has to be made in a similar way, with a similar set of information, but the significance and impact of the information will be different each day. However, if the delivery service was to the retail branches of the same chain of shops it might well be a fixed plan.

In routine decisions, information and experience in the use of the information with knowledge of the environment is important. In theory such a decision can be programmed; in reality it requires someone who is able to balance the information flow with experience. The system providing information for such decisions has to feed the decision-maker with the facts – computers can do a lot of the routine work – but only the decision-maker can decide to use or ignore the information.

Complex decisions

Decisions about long-term strategy and about people are usually complex and unpredictable. Previous experience is often of little direct value, as the decisions have never had to be made before. Similar decisions may have been made in the past, but this time the people and the times are different and so the decision-maker must start from scratch.

Because such decisions cannot be predicted, the information needs also cannot be predicted. This means that information systems that serve these windows of opportunity have to be more general. If specific information requirements are not known, then the decision-maker has to seek the information that is needed to make the decision. This places a particular strain on the information system. A good deal of information must be provided as and when it is needed, without knowing precisely when this is. This problem has given rise to the development of comprehensive computer databases holding vast amounts of

LIVERPOOL
JOHN MOORES UNIVERSITY
AVRIL ROBARTS LRC
TEL. 0151 231 4022

information, with facilities for management to access it when required. In principle this seems to be a good idea, but the cost and complexity involved are enormous.

In routine and complex decisions, the information needed – and the way it is used – depends to a large extent on the managers themselves, their attitudes, experiences, and personality.

History

There are two fallacies concerning history. The first is that people learn from it. The second is that we can base future decisions on it.

Historical information has a place, and that is in the past. Knowing how we got into the position we are in has little to do with how we go on from here. A great deal of management accounting information is concerned with history. Much of it is modern history, some is medieval, and yet more is prehistoric. What are we to do with all this history? To gauge performance over the immediate past (and for most organisations this seems to be a basic need) it is important to present the relevant information as soon after the period as possible. Then focus can turn to present performance and, most importantly, what measures are being taken with regard to future performance. Historical data is a record of what happened in the past but it is, of course, better to know what is happening *now*. It is important not to fall under the delusion that history has a bearing on future activity. Such delusion has led to the demise of many large organisations.

> ## The lost order
>
> 'Did you hear that we lost the big order for the new bypass?'
> 'No. What happened?'
> 'Well, it seems that we went in at our usual price and we were undercut by the opposition.'
> 'But we are so competitive, how could that be?'
> 'I don't know, but it happened.'
> 'So what are we doing about it?'
> 'Well, the boss has launched an enquiry as to what happened, and we are examining our pricing policy in detail.'
> 'And where do you think it will lead?'
> 'I'm not sure. What I am sure about is that we're going to look very closely at our prices on the new motorway job.'
> 'But I thought that was due in this week?'
> 'Yes it is, and we're making damn sure that we get this one.'

In this brief conversation, we can see that the information that is most important from the event, i.e. the failure to win the contract, is already being used as an impetus to act on the current event. But is an enquiry necessary?

Sometimes, reference to history is useful in avoiding difficulties in the future, but only when the same, or a very similar, set of circumstances are likely to occur. The danger is that by constantly looking back at what has happened we fail to keep our eye on the road ahead.

> **?**
>
> | **6.2 My windows of opportunity** |
> |---|
> | Make a list – under the three headings of mechanical, routine, and complex – of the decisions you take. Think about your working environment first and then about your life in general. You might find the outcome interesting. |

Information redundancy

Information becomes redundant for several reasons:

- the decision for which it was needed has been taken;
- it is past its sell-by date (it is too old);
- the transaction has been completed satisfactorily;
- the event or decision has been overtaken by new conditions;
- organisational change, i.e. new structures;
- new managers arrive and need different information;
- the role/job requirements change.

This is not an exhaustive list, but serves to show that information system infrastructure has to cope with the possibility of changing needs. It also has to accept information redundancy as a fact of life, and not as an inconvenience to the *status quo*.

Perhaps the final point on this topic is made by going back to the quote we started with:

'... for routine that serves a valuable purpose when initiated may cease to be useful by some later change in conditions.'

6.5 Data attributes

Data is the plural of *datum*. A datum is a fact, a name, a number, etc. In fact, although data is a Latin plural, it is now widely used as an aggregate singluar noun ('all the essential data *is* here...'), and it is used thus in this text. Without some qualifying label data does not have much value, so for it to be made use of data it has to exist in some meaningful relationship to other data.

Data is the raw material of information, and has to be collected and stored in a way that is meaningful to its subsequent use. To do this we have to understand a little more about the theory of data.

The nature of data

An item of data, also known as an attribute, has to exist in some meaningful context, outside which it is useless. For example, the name David Smith means nothing except that it can be assumed to refer to a person who exists. If more data – an address, say – is added, we have some context for the name, i.e. it is the person who lives at that address. It can also be assumed that David Smith is a man because we know that David is a man's name. But this is still not very meaningful. Adding a label to this data by, stating that David Smith is a customer, gives a context in which the data begin to have a meaning.

An item of data (attribute) is, then, a fact which has a single value – i.e. there is one David Smith, and one address where he lives. These items of data are at the lowest level of meaningful subdivision. The name could be split into first and second names, but unrelated they are meaningless.

Entities

An entity is the identifier of a class of data. It exists in relation to other entities. In the example above, David Smith is identified as a customer. 'Customer' is an entity of which there are many in the company. Another entity could be 'product', of which there are also many.

Entities have attributes, which for our example might be as follows:

Customer	*Product*
David Smith	D7103
37 Park Road	Green tiger
Surbiton	Large
Credit limit £5000	In stock 300

The usefulness of data occurs when we see entities in relationship with other entities.

Relationships

In creating a data model of the system we want to build it is important to correctly identify all the entities and the way they are related. This analysis results in an *entity-relationship diagram*. There are three levels that can exist, and these are shown in Figure 6.3.

Figure 6.3: Entity-relationship diagram

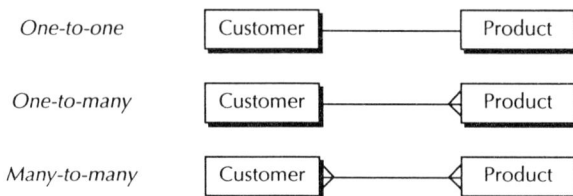

This way of representing relationships between entities is seen as a very good way of depicting the way that data can be structured to provide access to related data when specific decisions arise.

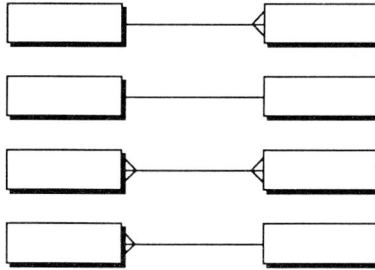

6.3 Relationahip levels

Produce examples of entities that would fit into the following relationships

Data-flow diagrams

Data-flow diagrams (DFDs) are another way of representing the data flows in an organisation. In this case an entity is represented as an oval, the data flow by an arrow, the process as a rectangle, and files (data stores) as parallel lines.

A simple DFD would appear as shown in Figure 6.4.

Figure 6.4: Data-flow diagram

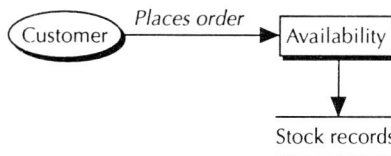

In this way every entity can be linked by data flows to the processes which use the data, stores of data, and other entities. The above – very simple – example could easily be extended to include product entities, and stores and delivery processes and entities.

One of the benefits of using entity-relationship diagrams and DFDs is the clarity they provide for subsequent systems design and construction of databases.

6.6 Data and file structures

A file is a collection of related data. A customer file might exist with data appertaining to customers; or a product file, with data relating to products. Within each of these files there would be records for each customer and each product respectively.

Each record would be made up of a number of fields, or data attributes. So the customer file could contain the following for each customer:

Customer No.   Name   Address   Credit terms   Credit status

The product file could hold:

Product No.   Description   Price   Quantity discount

Prior to computers it was probable that these records would have been stored in a meaningful sequence which, in the case of customers, might have been by customer number or customer name. If records were kept in the sequence of customer name, i.e. alphabetically, it would have required a time-consuming search if all that was available as an access key was the customer number. This could be circumvented by having a separate file containing:

Customer No.   Name

If this is the case then, in theory, the customer file need not contain the customer number attribute. Unfortunately, several customers could have the same name. Therefore, even if the search of the customer number file yielded the name, it would not be clear which of the several was the right one, unless other attributes, such as address, could be checked.

It is very important that every record in a file has a primary key attribute which is used for accessing that data record. This has to be unique so that it is impossible to access any other record when the key is used. Of course, there could be other attributes in the record which could be used as a key, but these will be secondary to the primary key.

These principles of data theory are very important in the construction of data records which can be accessed quickly and accurately for the data needed to create the information on which managers will base their decisions.

By way of metaphor,. imagine data storage as being a filing cabinet. In this metaphorical description the modern database terms are shown in brackets. Each cabinet is a data store (database), within which there are a series of files (tables). In each file there are records (rows), and each record is made up of data items, fields, or attributes (elements). To make use of the data store more effective there might also be a catalogue (data dictionary) of the contents for quick reference of data location.

The structure might appear as follows:

Figure 6.5: Data storage structure

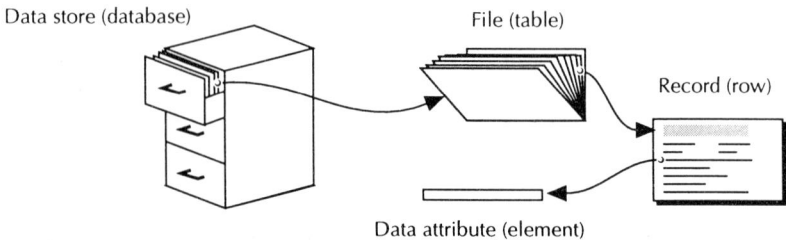

Data store (database)   File (table)   Record (row)

Data attribute (element)

The corresponding way of looking at the modern database equivalent is a reminder of the structure of most spreadsheets.

Figure 6.6: Spreadsheet structure

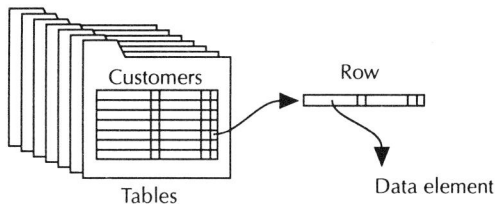

Database types

There are three main types of database structures in common use today: *hierarchical* databases, *network* databases and *relational* databases.

Hierarchical databases

These are the earliest form of database used on computers where data was held in a strict hierarchy similar to the organisation chart, or the family tree. In this structure the relationships were limited to one-to-one, and one-to-many. Each parent could have one or more children, but children could only have one parent. The hierarchy starts with a root node (parent) and branches from there to nodes (children), which might branch to further nodes and so on. Apart from the root node, which has no parent, nodes can be children of the node above, and parents of the nodes below them. An example is shown in Figure 6.7.

Figure 6.7: Hierarchical database

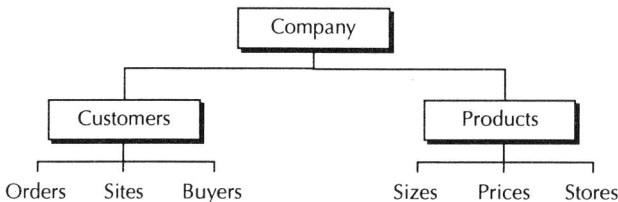

Access to data within this structure is possible only by following the structure down each branch. The usual access routine is from top to bottom and from left to right, which makes access slow. There are four main forms of access:

- *Sequential* (HSAM – hierarchical sequential access method) – which means going through the database in the sequence of its structure.
- *Indexed sequential* (HISAM) – which means having an index of where to go for certain data types, thus short-cutting the sequential mode.
- *Direct access* (HDAM – hierarchical direct access method) – which uses a

mechanism for giving each data type a physical address where it can be found on the database.

■ *Indexed direct access* (HIDAM) – which is an HDAM with an index.

Network databases

Network databases are structured to allow all three forms of relationship, i.e. one-to-one, one-to-many, and many-to-many. The paths through the database can be extremely varied, rather like a road map. Any data entity could have many parents and many children.

The structure still operates with files, records and data elements. It is formulated using a overall schema (the road map) and subschema (town street plans). Below this will be the sets of records. In this context 'sets' means data that have the same relationship with other data – not the mathematical meaning. Data is still held in tables and access is managed by the database management system, which knows from the schema and subschema where data is stored.

The terminology and standards for the operation of network databases were developed by a body called the Conference on Data Systems and Languages (CODASYL). Network database systems are often referred to as CODASYL systems.

Network databases are probably as flexible and comprehensive as any form of database. However, like hierarchical databases, they lack data independence and changes in the structure, e.g. deleting a parent, will mean changing the schema and application programs that access the database.

Relational databases

A relational database is a collection of related tables. The tables contain records (rows) that have the same attribute types. For example, taking our earlier idea of a customer file, a table can be represented as follows.

Customer no.	Name	Address	Credit terms	Credit status
657123	David Smith	37 Park Road Surbiton	14 days	BB
657134	Jones & Co	Unit 23 Western Estate Bristol	Monthly	BBB
657247	Wills Bros.	222 Main Street Wigan	14 days	A

This table may be related to another, which might hold records of sales invoices. One means of doing this is by a *join* which will create another table, combining the attributes from both tables, using a common attribute, e.g. customer number, as the link. This is an appropriate method of combining data when it will be accessed in a combined form regularly.

However, there is another way to combine tables which is suitable for *ad hoc* data requests. A *view* is created: it does not create a permanent new table, but creates a combined table only when data is accessed via the view. This invisible table, which does not exist in physical terms, is a very useful reporting device.

Perhaps the most important aspect of relational databases is data independence. When data is changed in a table, or a new table is introduced, there is no need to change any structure because, in effect, there is no structure to change. Nor is it necessary to change application programs. This makes relational databases both flexible and easily accessible. For example, a table might exist for employee name and address details with the employee number as the key. A second, related table holds pay rates with employee number as the key. When an employee is added, both tables can be updated through the data dictionary using the new employee number.

If a new table is introduced for a new bonus system (as long as it uses employee number and the data dictionary is amended to include the new table data) then no other changes are necessary.

So that is the basic theory of creating appropriate databases to enable data to be accessed in an appropriate way to produce the information needed for decision-making. It is fortunate that the technical aspects of databases can be left to the experts and that database management systems can be relied on to support the creation and use of databases.

6.7 Summary

- There is a basic systems theory which sees systems as organised sets of connected entities which have a purpose and can be open (receiving input and outputting into the environment) or closed (having no interaction with the environment).
- The state of information changes with time and circumstances.
- Information is only as valuable as the use to which it is put and in the way that it can reduce risk.
- Information is relevant when it impacts on decisions, and it rapidly becomes redundant.
- Data has relevance and value in terms of its particular attributes and relationship to other data.

7 Information Resources

7.1 Information overload

We have now reached the state of 'information overload'. There is, quite simply, too much information available. The point of diminishing returns, where additional information costs more to harvest than it is worth, has long been reached.

Figure 7.1: Diminishing returns

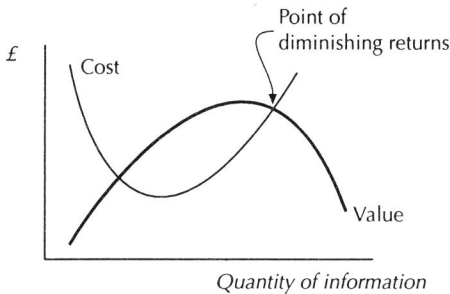

Quantity of information

Figure 7.1 shows the increasing cost of collecting, managing and accessing information as the amount of information managed grows, set against the value the information provides (see Chapter 8). A point is reached where the cost rises above the value.

The problem has been that, although the theory can be represented quite simply as a pair of lines on a graph, in reality there is a great deal of uncertainty about which information carries most value and is therefore most worthwhile gathering.

Needles and haystacks

Information is a resource when it can be used directly to aid decision-making and to add value to the activities of the organisation. Databases provide a way in which information can be stored, managed and accessed. The problem with databases is that the way the information is to be used has to be considered in the construction of the database. This then limits their value for storing the vast amounts of data now available and for which there may not be a predefined use. This is like looking for the needle of pertinent fact in the haystack of data. Fortunately, data warehousing has arrived, although there are mixed reactions to its value. At one extreme is the view that this is the 'best thing since sliced bread'; at the other, the view that it is a waste of time, money and effort. A good starting point is a brief description of a data warehouse.

A data warehouse can best be described as a dedicated computer that stores vast amounts of data and which has the power to sort through this data very quickly. Data warehouses are repositories of data that is placed in the data warehouse because it may have some value to the business. Unlike databases, which support active operating systems and where data changes dynamically in a predefined way, data warehouses are refreshed at intervals with additional data so that the amount of data stored grows. The main problem with data warehouses has been to make sense of this mass of data. It is possible to establish searches according to sets of variables and to produce reports, but with so many variables and so much data it is difficult to know which particular sets are valuable.

The answer to this problem is data mining, using new types of intelligent software which search through data looking for patterns. This is an enormous leap forward compared to the hit-and-miss human selection of what might be important. As an example, consider data collected by retail stores from shoppers. The amount of data involved in recording every shopper's purchases on every visit to the store is immense – what they buy, when they buy it, how often they buy it, how it relates to their customer profile (collected from the data provided by customers when they sign up for storecards). All this data can now be stored in a data warehouse and mined for its value by using a data-mining tool to establish meaningful patterns. The outcomes can affect direct promotions, in-store displays, product ranges, pricing patterns and many other aspects that arise from understanding shoppers' behaviour.

In organisations that have large numbers of debtors, data on buying and payment patterns can signal potential bad debts well in advance of the customer defaulting.

Subtle changes in the way the customer operates may be highlighted by the data-mining tool when the human equivalent might not have noticed the pattern until it was too late.

Data on customer behaviour may also indicate customers who are preparing to move to a competitor. For example, if order quantities decline slightly, this might indicate that the customer is buying some of his needs elsewhere to test quality of service, etc. before switching completely. It is these subtle patterns hidden in the data that could make an enormous difference to all kinds of strategic decision-making. The problem is that the benefits are unknown until the data warehouse has been created and data mining started.

The big difference with data warehouses is that it is not necessary – in fact it limits the system – if data is stored according to specific criteria. In normal databases it is the specificity of data that enables it to be located speedily. In data warehouses it is preferable to allow the data-mining tools to search in an unspecified way for patterns. The tools can be asked questions to see if a perceived pattern exists and has any meaning, but they work best when allowed to mine on their own.

In looking for patterns, humans can handle only a small number of variables, possibly as low as eight. Machines can handle hundreds or thousands. Yet – and this is the crunch – because they are only machines, even with the power to handle enormous volumes, they may come up with useless patterns: people over the age of 60 do not buy computer games, for example. Somewhere along the line, then, people have to study the outcomes and retrain the software tools to recognise what might be significant for their particular organisation.

A suitable analogy would be prospecting for gold: people go prospecting to see if the geology supports the possibility of 'gold in them there hills'. The likelihood of striking it rich at the first attempt is remote, and the mining or prospecting software is most likely to produce a great deal of waste to go with the occasional nugget. However, for large organisations where data volumes can run to trillions of bytes, the discovery of the occasional nugget can be of immense value.

One US bank analysed more than 100,000 loans to find the criteria that would indicate which type of loan would generate the most profit. The rules that were defined involved combinations of variables beyond what any human mind could figure out.

So how can an organisation decide whether data warehousing and data mining might be of use? There are really only four questions for managers to ask.

- Are we in the business of selling many products to many customers from many places, or do we provide a limited number of services to millions of customers, and does the combination of variables and the volume of data exceed what can be handled any other way?
- Do we have the money available to make the investment without being able to calculate any payoff?
- Do we have the skills to harness the data warehousing and data-mining technology for the benefit of the business?
- Do we have efficient operational systems that will produce the data in all its possible variations for transfer into the data warehouse?

Data warehouse and data mining are at the moment the preserve of very big organisations where the investment, which can run into millions of pounds, is worthwhile in terms of, say, percentage of profits or cost per customer. What is certain to happen is that the technology will improve and the costs will fall, putting data warehousing and data mining in the hands of much smaller businesses where, even though data volumes are smaller, the benefits can still be considerable. One such business, a medium-sized Australian insurance company, is developing data warehousing to enable it to provide large industrial customers with information on their claims history in such a way that premiums can be adjusted to reflect the profitability of different policies with different types of risks and different types of customers. Not a new approach, but with data mining the combinations of variables can be so extensive in arriving at a suitable set of criteria that the company thinks its investment will pay off in terms of keeping existing customers and providing them with a powerful competitive edge to win new customers.

Once again, as with any technology, the answer lies in the successful application of the new capabilities. There are very few businesses that can just 'suck it and see', so perhaps the best advice is to wait for a year or so to see what happens. During this time the hype will give way to real examples of successful applications and the costs will fall. There is a price to pay for being on the bandwagon, and a price to pay for lagging too far behind.

It is also important to remember that data warehouses do not replace operational databases. They are an extra that depends on getting detailed and accurate data about the businesses activities and the customers the business serves. This might mean finding our much more about customers than is known at the present time. The discounts and facilities offered with loyalty cards and storecards are a small price to pay for such detailed information.

7.2 Decision-related information

Part III of this book covers in depth the subject of information for decision-making. This section focuses on the idea of using information as a resource, by picking up information that is directly related to the decisions that people make. This information can be separated into four categories.

- *Information about the decision and the need for the decision.* For example, what has given rise to the need for this decision? Is this a routine decision or one that is taken infrequently?
- *Information about who takes the decision.* Is the decision made by more than one person? Is decision responsibility unclear?
- *Information about the importance of the decision on the organisation and its activities.* What impact does it have?
- *Information about the outcomes of the decision after the decision has been made.* What can be learned from our decision-making experience?

All this information can be gathered and can directly help people to understand the nature of decisions and decision-making in their organisations. Too little is known and understood about decision-making in most organisations, and considerable value could be derived from more information about decisions and decision-making.

Prioritising information

It is difficult to prioritise information if decisions and decision-making are not well understood. We can take an example of a decision and explore this in more detail.

Hit-and-miss quarrying

A dry-stone quarry manager has to decide the number of vehicles he needs to hire for the next day. He has to take this decision at 5.00 p.m. By this time approximately 80 per cent of the orders for the next day have been received. From past experience, the quarry manager has arrived at a simple average workload for a vehicle as four 20-tonne loads a day. To order the vehicles the manager divides by 80 the total tonnage ordered and books the vehicles.

The precise calculation depends on the distance, the quantity, the material, and the time it takes to load and unload, as well as the vagaries of particular customers and the weather. Depending on the time of year the traffic can have a significant effect, as can roadworks and accidents. Vehicle breakdowns can cause a problem, as can production problems. The known and the unknown jockey for position in the decision process. In the end the priority information is the quantity ordered, and the decision-making formula is:

$$\frac{\text{Total tonnage ordered}}{80} + 2$$

This simple formula has worked, more or less, for many years and serves to produce some days of excellent vehicle utilisation and some days of very poor vehicle utilisation.

In the scenario above the priority information is chosen because of the ease of acquiring it within the timescale of the decision, i.e. by 5.00 p.m. and because it provides an outcome which, on average, approximates to a satisfactory result. It could be argued that this is not the best answer and that more information should be included in the formula, so that a more 'accurate' number of vehicles could be ordered. A simple computer model would certainly allow for a number of 'what ifs' before the decision is taken – but would the time and cost involved make it worthwhile?

Prioritisation of information is based on usefulness and confidence in a reasonable outcome, rather than precision and accuracy. This depends upon experience in both decision-making and the nature of the information that is available.

Accessing information

The best time to access information is the moment when the decision has to be taken. At this point the information has the potential to influence the decision. Any earlier and the information may be 'stale', any later and the information will have no impact, except to feed 'hindsight'. Because timing is such a crucial ingredient of the decision-making process, methods for accessing information have to be well thought through and built into the information systems infrastructure.

This can be done in a variety of ways.

> ## Concrete facts
>
> Two production managers, who are responsible for the northern and western regions of a large readymix concrete company, have their own ways of accessing the information they need to manage production. The manager of the northern region employs a production clerk who regularly gathers information on his PC from the fifteen plants in his region. His manager, who travels constantly around the region, is able to phone in from his mobile phone and ask for the information he needs. If there is an emergency, his production clerk can contact him directly. The northern production manager is well known for always being where he is needed.
>
> The manager of the western region prefers to use his own laptop computer to gather the information from his sixteen plants. He talks about having his information at his fingertips. He spends about half his time in his office and about half visiting his plants. He maintains that he needs only be where the problems are and that he can tell this from the information he assembles on his computer. He also has a mobile phone and plant managers can contact him if they need to.
>
> Both managers have very good reputations for meeting production targets, for minimising the impact of production problems and for managing their people.

Accessing information is not just about the technology that is used, it is also about knowing what information is required. It is this aspect of information management that relies so heavily on experience, not in information management, but in the decision-making process for which the information is used.

Successfully accessing the information required depends on the following:

- knowing what information is required;
- knowing where to find it;
- knowing how to access it;
- being able to respond appropriately when the information is available; and
- knowing when the information no longer has value and being able to discard it.

7.3 Protecting a valuable resource

Information that has been painstakingly collected and stored, so that it can be accessed by those who need it, has a significant value. This value has to be protected. The protection of information is concerned with four main issues.

- *Allowing only those who need it and are authorised to receive it to access it*
  Limiting access to information protects the information and its use and serves to 'close' the freedom of information. Organisations seeking to operate an 'open' information approach will find that limiting access will soon lead to a closed system as more and more limits are placed on who can access what. Perhaps one way round this is to operate an open approach to accessing the

main databases and to allow individuals to create their own 'closed' files for their own use. Another approach is to allow access to 'read-only' files on the database, and so limit the extraction of information.

- *Ensuring that it is complete and correct*
  As data flows into the database it is important to establish system checks which ensure that it is complete and correct.

  Complete data means that all the data is present. For example, for a retail chain of shops it might be that every branch has sent in the data for a particular week. A set of invoices will be complete if the invoice-numbering sequence is complete – there are no missing invoice numbers.

  Correct data means that the content of the data is realistic, fits within certain ranges, is arithmetically accurate, and that the detail transactions agree with the control totals. All these checks should be system-based, and reports produced on any discrepancies found, with subsequent checks to see that the discrepancies have been corrected.

- *Ensuring that it is not allowed to deteriorate with use and over time*
  Information deteriorates over time and with use. The time factor is easy to understand and affects different information in different ways. Some information has a very short life span, some a very long life span. Examples of information with a short life span would be the racing form information for an afternoon's racing or the short-range weather forecast. Examples of information with a long life span would be a mathematical formula, or a cookery recipe.

  Deterioration of information with use is less easy to appreciate. It happens when information is used in such a way that it becomes 'fixed' in the minds of decision-makers. An example of this (from the scenario earlier in this chapter) would be the formula used by the quarry manager to order vehicles. If vehicle sizes changed so that vehicles could carry 30 tonnes, the old formula ought to be changed. Another example would be the standard cost of production of a component that is used in an estimating procedure which is not changed when the component is manufactured in larger quantities, or when the component design is changed.

  These examples could be seen as oversights on the part of the managers concerned, and they can be seen as the continued use of information that has deteriorated in value. This means that the use of information should be constantly evaluated to ensure that the latest and the best information is being used for decision-making.

- *Preventing its deliberate or accidental loss and/or corruption*
  Information can be lost and/or corrupted when it is accessed and amended and/or deleted, or when the system has inappropriate checks and controls. This can be minimised, i.e. the information protected, by limiting the type of people who can adjust the information held on file. In addition, the recording of all changes that are made, and the continued storage of the old data – at least for an agreed period of time – can help to protect the information's integrity.

The whole question of information protection brings into focus the need for carefully designed and well-policed systems for security and control of information, especially in information infrastructures where information flows relatively freely along the networks that serve the organisation.

7.4 Summary

- Finding information among data is like searching for needles in a haystack.
- Fortunately modern software tools can help us to mine vast quantities of data for information which might have meaning.
- Part of this process of finding useful information is to know what is being sought, or to be able to prioritise what is needed so that the most useful information can be sought first. Sometimes what is 'most useful' is not known.
- Once information has been found it must be maintained and protected.

8 The Value of Information

8.1 Information is a vital resource

Information is vital to effective business management. Knowing what is happening, where and when, and its effects on the business is essential. This can be achieved only if managers have been able to clearly define and express their needs and that information providers have understood these needs. There are many problems in doing this successfully, not least of which is the extent to which organisations become systems-dependent.

No other resource has been subject to the technological advances of information processing and communications during the last twenty years. The expenditure in human effort has been vast and the rewards equally large. The impact on daily life has been dramatic. Yet we are still at an elementary stage in the efficient use of this vital and valuable resource.

Living without information

Even the most primitive man relied on information to survive. To consider survival without information is akin to thinking of surviving without food, water and protection. Information is collected via the senses: touch, taste, smell, hearing and sight. These five senses feed information to the brain about current surroundings. Of all the animals, only humans have developed the ability to communicate beyond the range of sight and hearing.

The earliest developments in communications – smoke signals and drums – made it possible for the range of human communication to be extended, but everything still depended on the ability to see and hear. Communication by means of sound and sight was very efficient over short distances, but beyond this range messages moved much more slowly.

Early merchants really were 'adventurers', people not knowing whether their voyage was a success or not until the ship returned – or not – many months later. Gradually, information began to move more quickly: as the speed of physical movement increased, so did the speed of information. The developments continued via the telegraph and the telephone, and information now travels so fast that events can be monitored as they happen, anywhere on the planet.

Survival

The primary reason for this tremendous advance has been self-preservation. Knowing who our enemies are, where they are, their numbers and weapons are basic to our survival Modern intelligence systems are based on discovering this information, albeit in a much more sophisticated way than our ancestors. Such information is of value only if it is available before the attack. It is useless to find out after the battle, even if it helps to show why it was lost. So speed is of the essence, and hence the sophisticated systems that have been developed have all concentrated on speed of collection and dissemination of information.

This basic need for survival has a commercial context, in the need to react to the activities of competitors and to be quick in responding to market reactions to new products and ideas.

8.2 Risk

There is always an element of risk that the outcomes of decisions taken will not be what was hoped or expected. Some outcomes may be predictable – for example, failure to fuel a fire will cause it to go out. Others are less predictable – for example, the success of a new product launch. Testing the market, or carrying out market research, i.e. gathering more information, can reduce such commercial risk, but it cannot be eliminated.

It is clear that information collected and communicated at the appropriate time can reduce risk, but to what extent is this true and is there a point where more information is unhelpful? The balance between what is necessary and what is enough is not easy to decide. Sometimes an extra piece of information might have changed the decision and the outcome. One way to try to achieve balance is to attempt to determine what information is needed for each decision taken. This in turn has to be related to the cost of providing the information.

There is no clear proof that more information leads to better decisions, and there are examples of both success and failure in situations where information is readily available and in others where it is not. Information is a vital resource, but improving the quality and quantity will create value only if it is used effectively. Just as with any other resource, information can be wasted.

8.3 The value of information

It is not easy to place a quantifiable value on information. As has been seen, the value depends on the use that can be made of the information and how it might reduce risk. It appears, however, that modern organisations place a high value on information. The development of sophisticated computer-based information systems implies that the output is considered to be of value.

Cost–benefit premiums

A large insurance company made the decision to embark on a major new information system development for three reasons:

- to maintain their position in the market, i.e. to protect their market share;
- to improve their information service to customers, which they believed would improve their competitive edge;
- to provide faster, more accurate information to managers on the success of their business activities, and hence focus on the most lucrative business.

To support the proposal a report was produced which showed the financial benefit emanating from these three outcomes. This was, of course, significantly higher than the proposed investment and so the project was approved.

In this scenario the value of the information could be expressed in very clear business terms. However, the real value is assessable only when the outcomes have been achieved and the investment can be seen to have been worthwhile.

8.4 The cost of information

It is much easier to say what information costs. Most organisations keep cost records for the activities that contribute to the provision of information. As computer use has become more widespread in organisations and networks have been introduced, the cost of 'the' information system has become harder to arrive at. However, it is still possible to arrive at a figure for 'information costs', and it can be a very large figure.

There are several areas of cost that have to be taken into account:

- the cost of the physical infrastructure, i.e. hardware, software, telephony, networks, etc.;
- the 'people cost' of those providing and maintaining the infrastructure;
- licences and contracts for developing and adapting proprietary systems;
- the costs of ensuring the integrity and security of the systems, including the procedures, the people and systems audit;
- the costs of the time and effort of users in helping to develop and learning to use the information systems.

In all these areas costs are increasing as organisations seek to produce more information and move it around more quickly. Information is becoming one of the most expensive resources of business activity. Management's demand for information appears insatiable. No sooner has one demand been met than another arises. The main problem is that it is not possible to place a clear value on meeting these needs, and so a reliable model cannot be constructed to help make decisions about the real value of providing more information.

Practical experiments are difficult to arrange. Few, if any, organisations would be willing for some managers to make decisions with limited information and others to make decisions with as much information as possible, and then measure the relative results. Experiments have been carried out in the form of management games, where teams are able to buy additional information, but these are by no means conclusive, and operating on a hunch seems just as successful as the very best-informed decisions. At the end of the day, what seems to be most valuable is the skill with which managers use the information they have. This takes us into a whole new area in the quest to find out how valuable information really is and whether or not dependency on information systems is a good thing.

8.5 Systems dependency

Organisations do not suddenly become dependent on information systems. The *realisation* that they are dependent comes suddenly, but the *growth* of dependency is a hidden process that will have been going on for some time. Most organisations take their information system infrastructure for granted, which is both foolhardy and dangerous.

The world is becoming more and more dependent on technology. Trying to exist without computers, at least in the western world, is a frightening concept; people would lose control. Traffic in many cities would become gridlocked, hospitals could not function, transport systems would be in chaos, and the banking system would collapse.

The world's top organisations, in terms of size and profitability, are now technology companies. The Internet is creating new markets and new forms of dependency. This is good for the providers, just as drug-pushers have realised there is much to be gained from dependency.

Managers have always been dependent to some degree on information. The difference now is that they have become dependent on the system.

The tail wagging the dog

Most organisations need to ask: 'Who decides the way we do things here?'

Do as you are told

A decision was taken to install a new computer-based production control system. The new system produced weekly production schedules from orders as they were received by exploding requirements into sub-assemblies and components, then checking these with current production schedules and stores levels. Everything worked well until it was realised that managers no longer had control of delivery dates, which the computer calculated. Managers could no longer switch priorities. Delivery dates lengthened and orders fell off. The system was checked and a fault traced to the stock levels and order quantities that had not been adjusted for increased demand. The chairperson reported that a major customer had asked her: 'How long have you been run by a computer then?'

Decision thrombosis

The new information system appeared very effective. Regular reports were being produced with more relevant information on market conditions than ever before. If special information was required this was available by using the local PCs. The opinion of most people was that the system was a vast improvement on the old one. It was a surprise, therefore, when the local director received a telephone call from an irate customer: 'I have been waiting for your quotation for two weeks now; what is the problem?' The director did not know, and said he would ring back. On checking he discovered that the system was 'down', so it was not possible to extract the relevant information on current costs and demand levels in order to produce the quotation. 'Didn't we used to keep a price schedule?' he asked. 'Yes,' came the reply, 'but when we changed to the new system we abandoned the old one.' The immediate problem was resolved by some 'informed' guesswork, and the old system of maintaining a current price schedule reintroduced as a stand-by.

Leaking systems

The new sales accounting system had been in operation for three months when a customer wrote asking why he had not received any invoices. On checking the system it was discovered that the particular product concerned was coded 1107. The product code field now being used contained only three digits, and the system had been ignoring all products with a code of more than three digits. The system was not programmed to reject and report the four-digit codes: the programmer had not expected any. After some work checking the orders and sales analysis, which both included the four-digit codes, the sales were identified and invoiced.

Fortunately an honest customer had triggered a review of the system and the leak was found. It could have gone on for much longer. Such leaks occur but faith in the system's infallibility seems to cloud common sense. All computer systems can – and do – fail.

We need two in case one fails

System failure is often countered by the provision of a second system, which comes into operation as soon as the main system fails. Such an approach, though expensive, is essential when the organisation is dependent on its computer systems. Sometimes the apparent surplus capacity of the stand-by machine is used for non-urgent and development work until it is no longer available as a stand-by. In one example, certain components from the stand-by system had been used by a maintenance engineer to keep the main machine running, thus destroying the whole point of having a stand-by.

> ## No-credit account
>
> In a large building society the new system was being evaluated for maintenance and stand-by requirements. The analysis indicated that on average a PC would fail three times in a year, a printer four times, a server twice, the local LAN three times, the network three times, and the central computers twice. With five hundred branches, the expected performance looked like this:
>
> - all branches off-line at least five times a year;
> - eight branches non-functional every day because of failed LANs;
> - five branches non-functional every day because of failed servers;
> - ten branches with printer problems every day; and
> - twenty-three branches with PC problems every day.

Road blocks and diversions

One of the problems of systems dependency is that it can dictate the direction of the business. The rigidity of many systems means that quite simple tasks sometimes have to travel tortuous routes through the system.

> ## Spouse grouse
>
> 'I have opened a new account in my maiden name and I would like to change it to my married name.'
>
> 'OK, what we need to do is to close the old account and to open a new one.'
>
> 'I don't want to do that, I just want to change the name on my account.' 'Well I'm sorry, but we can't do that. The system doesn't allows us to change account names and signatures.'
>
> 'But I'm going to use the same signature, I just want to change the name.' 'What if I go through the process and do it for you? I have all the details: all I need is for you to fill in the top of this form stating the name you want the account opened in. Of course, you will have to provide me with some form of identification with your married name and your current address.'
>
> 'For goodness sake, I'll leave it. Don't bother.'

The traffic jam

One of the problems with networks is the traffic that flows along the lines, and the way in which the system handles traffic jams by rerouting data. Just like the road system, entering the system at the wrong time can lead to becoming stuck in a traffic jam. By scheduling work and prioritising data packages so that high-priority data can flow straight through, it is possible to keep the traffic moving. Another answer is new lines with wider bandwidths and faster transfer speeds, essential for multimedia transmissions.

The final solution

As the third millennium approaches the implications of systems dependency and the value of information are to be widely tested. As the year 2000 looms up ahead of us the question of whether computers will continue to function has to be answered. The problem is easy to state, and much more difficult to correct.

Many old computer systems use a two-digit date field, which much software will not be able to handle when the date changes from 1999 ('99' in two-digit form) to 2000 ('00'). The first snag is that most programs will not accept 00 as a valid year and, even if they do, they will not know if it is 1900 or 2000; the second is the question of whether 00 comes before or after 99. The tax year 99/00 will cause untold problems! Programs will cease to work and systems will crash.

Can it be that bad? Yes it can, and it has been estimated that the worldwide bill for fixing computer programs before 31 December 1999 will exceed £400 billion. The value of information systems and the data they contain is staggering. This is going to be the big test.

For each organisation the questions to be asked are not, 'Do we have a problem?' but 'What is the size of the problem?' and 'How are we going to deal with it?' There are perhaps three approaches that can be followed.

- Find every single program that uses a date field and reprogram to fix it.
- Replace all software with new software that will cope with the problem.
- A mixture of the two.

The answer in each case will depend on the size of the problem and the time, effort and resources needed to fix it. Even this is more difficult than it sounds because the documentation for many old 'legacy' systems either does not exist or has not been kept up to date. Users of proprietary packages may discover that their licences run out on 31 December 1999. They will need to negotiate licences for 2000. Some people will make a lot of money out of this; some will lose a lot.

Many organisations have been working on the problem for some years and will be ready. Others are only beginning to appreciate the problem and may find that the systems that they relied on are under threat. This is the problem of systems dependency. The value lies in the continuing availability of the systems and the information they contain, and the extent of the value is recognised only when the possibility of losing it all is considered.

8.6 Summary

- Information has value in relation to its usefulness. This usually means in terms of the reduced risk or advantage it provides in decision-making.
- Information also has a cost, and some costs more than it will ever repay.
- Becoming dependent on information systems is a danger that has to be evaluated. Dependency may not be avoidable but it is important to be aware of the extent to which the organisation is dependent.

PART III
Information for
Decision-making

Part III is about using information effectively and starts in Chapter 9 by making the link, between information and decision-making, which is fundamental to the concept of the 'informed manager'. Chapter 10 contains a strong argument for presenting information effectively and makes the case for 'relevance reporting', where the focus is on highlighting the 'specific' information that is needed.

Much of being informed is concerned with how data is converted into information by relating it to the events and circumstances of individual decisions. This important point reinforced by Chapters 11, 12, and 13 which look at particular examples of modelling (spreadsheets) to bring together and display information in a way that directly feeds into the decision-making process. The widespread use of PCs makes spreadsheet modelling available to all, yet skill in formulating and constructing models effectively is not widespread.

The final chapter in the book looks at executive information systems (EIS) and how these can be used to create the 'informed manager'. Once again it has to be said that EIS tools are effective only if managers know the information they want and the use to which they want to put it.

The whole of Part III is aimed at showing that using information effectively is not a passive process – where managers sit back and wait for information to be presented to them – but much more an interactive one, where managers go out to get the information they need and assist in constructing the systems they require to be truly 'informed'.

9 Information for Decision-making

9.1 Critical success factors

Success in the application of information management can be measured only in terms of the success of the organisation in using information to achieve its strategic objectives. It is therefore essential for the organisation to create an appropriate information management strategy and the systems infrastructure to support it. Appropriate, because it has to provide for the culture of the organisation as well as the way that work and relationships are organised.

A major obstacle towards achieving this is that many information management strategies today are conceived, described and classified in terms of the technology itself, e.g. computers, communications and software. They need instead to be described in terms of the management processes which they are intended to serve.

If driven by technological opportunities the strategy produces systems which are operationally effective, but ineffective in terms of achieving business benefits. This can result in computer terminals with advanced capabilities in undisciplined and unprepared production environments, and reports lying unused on the desks of unreceptive users.

There is a history of the use and misuse of computers, but it is questionable if anything can be learnt from it. This is because the history is mainly about projects concerning large mainframe systems, involving large teams of experts, and taking many months or years to complete. This is not today's computer environment. To look back on what has happened will only serve to confuse: we must look forward to what has to be done.

The critical factors of success lie in four distinctly separate but related areas: technologies, information structures, business needs, and people.

Technology factors

Technology can be considered as three closely knit areas: computers, communications, and software. In all these areas the key factors are:

- technical skills to maintain operationally effective services;
- technical expertise to select and implement the most appropriate infrastructures;
- keeping a watchful eye on changing technologies and assessing opportunities as they arise;

- provision of a consultancy-style service to management;
- dismantling of ivory towers and the dogmas they contain;
- avoidance of 'technology push' in favour of meeting business needs;
- for technology specialists, being as willing to learn about business as they are to teach about technology.

Information factors

Although the need for relevant information has always been recognised, the realisation of the ideal has been severely restricted by the limitations of the mechanisms for achieving it. With the removal of these limitations by modern technology further obstacles have arisen. For example:

- meeting varying information needs in different parts of the business;
- the avoidance of duplication, ambiguity, and inconsistency;
- deciding who owns the data and controls its use;
- defining information needs effectively.

These obstacles can be overcome. The key factors in achieving this are:

- acceptance of the need for specific applications to meet specific needs of departments and individuals;
- increasing the information awareness of people at all levels of the organisation;
- providing a method for ensuring good-quality information;
- encouraging an attitude of group working and sharing of information;
- providing a new view of information management which is not centred on the technological infrastructure, but on the information it produces.

Business needs

All businesses need systems for enacting the business from which they extract a profit. These systems are a mixture of formality and informality, normal practice and exception, people, paper and machines. In some businesses there is a great deal of formalisation and stability; in others change and innovation are the order of the day. So needs vary. The key factors of success in meeting business needs are:

- establishing the most effective systems environment for the business;
- clarifying the needs for information at three levels: operational, planning and control;
- identifying the individual, department, division, and company performance indicators;
- specifying the decision-based information needs of managers at all levels;
- focusing attention on business performance.

People factors

Today it is widely recognised that there is a dependence on skilled people with the right attitudes to make systems work, to maintain information integrity, and to be opportunity-seeking in their work. This means that the new challenges this brings in motivation, training, management and working relationships must also be recognised.

To be successful in the 'people' area attention must be paid to these key factors:

- the need to overcome 'technofear';
- balancing technology enthusiasm, which is the other side of the technofear coin;
- ensuring that people take ownership of all the information aspects of their work;
- providing appropriate training, support and coaching with the focus on individual performance;
- encouraging and welcoming change at all levels and in all areas of business activity.

In all four areas of concern it is important to recognise the role that managers play in ensuring success. No longer is the development of effective systems the prerogative of the specialists. Today managers play a vital role in ensuring that systems meet their needs in the way that they want them to, not in a way dictated by specialists to make life easier for themselves.

The decision

'I have to have your decision today Joe, I'm sorry but that's how it has to be.'

Joe sat and pondered his dilemma. He was pretty sure he knew what he wanted to do, but he felt he could just not finalise his decision until he had the information about the latest order levels.

'Bill, I still haven't got the latest order level figures – what's going on?'

Bill, the DP manager, was well aware of the problem, but he wasn't going to let Joe know that they had had a disk crash and were having to rerun the data for the last two weeks.

'OK Joe, I realise we're running late, but I hope to have the figures ready by later today.'

Joe wasn't convinced that he would get the figures so he rang Michelle, the marketing manager.

'Michelle, it's Joe here. Can you help me with the up-to-date order levels? I need to know to decide about the supplies of parts for the next three months.'

'You should have the full report by now. What's happening?'

'Well, Bill tells me he should have them later today, but I doubt if he will. You must have some idea.'   *Continued over...*

> ### The decision
>
> 'Well, I can give you our current totals for each product group, but I don't have them divided into product types.'
>
> 'OK, could you let me have them as soon as possible please?'
>
> 'Yes, alright, I'll send you a fax. It will take about ten minutes.'
>
> A little later Joe was looking at the fax. He could see all he wanted to know from the group totals and soon arrived at his decision. It wouldn't matter within five or ten per cent how accurate he was as long as he didn't under-order. He made his phone call and placed his order. At 5.15 p.m., just before Joe left his office, Bill rang.
>
> 'I'm sorry Joe but it will be tomorrow midday at the earliest before you get the figures.'
>
> 'OK Bill, I'll just have to manage without them then, won't I?' was Joe's laconic reply.

There are several important elements in this scenario in terms of matching business needs with information resources. See if you can identify the key points.

> ### 9.1 My information needs
>
> Select one of the areas where you are responsible for making a decision, or think of a decision which someone else takes, but with which you are familiar. Now decide for this decision what information you:
>
> (a) must have;
> (b) should have;
> (c) would like to have.

9.2 Performance indicators

If critical success factors (CSFs) are those activities or areas of work to which particular attention must be paid, then performance indicators (PIs) are measures used to determine how well the CSFs are performed.

Information is, of course, an essential ingredient in measuring performance. Yet without PIs it becomes very difficult to select information to assess performance. This demands that an information strategy is developed to provide information in relation to the CSFs and which focuses directly on the performance indicators.

In every individual's job, in every departmental activity, in every business unit, in every company, there will be at least three critical success factors which need to be focused on. Defining what these are at every level is one of the keys to creating a successful information strategy. It could be argued that there are more than three: indeed there are, but we are concerned with the three that really matter. The rest will be secondary.

❓ | 9.2 My three critical success factors

Write down your three critical success factors in the space below.

CSF 1:

CSF 2:

CSF 3:

Defining performance indicators

Whichever CSF is being focused on there will be some indicator that the CSF has been performed to the desired level. Take an example of a CSF for credit control. The primary performance indicator might be the average number of days taken by debtors to pay. Another PI might be the percentage of debtors above 90 days. These might be set as:

- Average days taken: PI = 35
- Percentage of debtors above 90 days: PI = 3%

❓ | 9.3 Performance indicators

Now, for each of the CSFs you listed in exercise 9.2, consider one or more PIs that might be appropriate.

CSF 1: PI =

CSF 2: PI =

CSF 3: PI =

There are many ways in which PIs can be expressed, from specific time and quantity measures to more subjective measures such as satisfaction and pleasure. But no matter how these indicators are set it should be clear and unequivocal that they have been achieved. PIs are often used as objectives, but this is not always helpful. For example, profit might be seen as a performance indicator, but it is *not* a CSF. Profit is the outcome of achieving other activity CSFs. A CSF is what is aimed for, a PI shows how well it is achieved.

The high jump

'You know David, that was your best jump yet.'

'But I hit the bar,' David replied.

'Yes, but you were so close. I think if we concentrate on your fitness for the next two weeks, and then tidy up your technique, we should be OK for the championships.'

'You mean I'll be able to clear 2.20?'

'I don't see why not, but let's take it a step at a time.'

A few weeks later, after the regional finals, David and his coach were discussing progress.

'So tell me what happened at the finals.'

'Well, I was going great then I just seemed to lose it,' David answered.

'What happened?'

'All my energy seemed to drain away, I just lost my edge,' David responded.

'OK, this is what I saw. You were pushing hard and seemed to put everything into the third jump at 2.15. It was a hot day, and I could see you were tiring, and I'm not surprised. It seemed to me that after the great jump at 2.15 your stamina gave out, and maybe your self-belief wavered.'

'Yeah, well, that seems a pretty accurate assessment,' David said with a grimace. 'So what now?'

'Well, here's how I rate your last performance – strength 9, technique 9, commitment 9, stamina 6, confidence 8, self-belief 6. Do you agree?'

'OK, so where do we go next?' David asked.

'I think we need to build up your stamina, then jump a few 2.20s to build up your self-belief, because I know you can do it.'

9.4 Separating CSFs and PIs

In the above scenario, objectives and performance indicators are both involved in the discussion. Can you separate them out and state what the objectives are, and what the performance indicators are?

The systems strategy survey

This survey follows a series of steps.

(i) *Activity analysis.* This analysis seeks to establish the key business activities. It divides the business into logical strategic business units, each of which is attacking specific markets with clearly identified products. Within each of these units there is usually a number of key business activities which need to be defined.

(ii) *Decision analysis.* Next, the decision-making that takes place in each activity is examined. Decisions are clearly identified and separated into categories: mechanical, routine, and complex.

(iii) *Information needs analysis.* In this step information is related to the decisions identified. This leads to the development of a set of information requirements related to individual business activities.

(iv) *Information levels.* The information requirements are categorised into three primary levels: operational, planning and control. Then the frequency and quality of the information can be assessed.

(v) *Data flows.* In order for information to be created data has to be collected, processed, stored and disseminated. This step in the survey determines how the data flows have to be organised.

(vi) *Systems framework.* With all this information to hand it is possible to construct a systems framework, which has to be created to meet the information needs of the business.

9.3 Decision support systems

A decision support system is a system which provides decision-makers with the information they need, in a supportive environment, to enable them to make decisions quickly and effectively.

The need for support

Figure 9.1 Supporting decision-makers

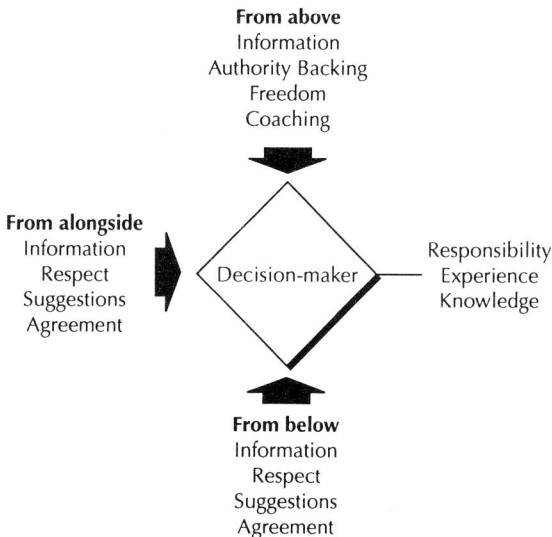

From above
Information
Authority Backing
Freedom
Coaching

From alongside
Information
Respect
Suggestions
Agreement

Decision-maker

Responsibility
Experience
Knowledge

From below
Information
Respect
Suggestions
Agreement

Many managers operate in a self-created zone of independent isolation. This comes about firstly as a form of self-protection, and secondly as a means of avoiding stumbling into other peoples' territory. The manager as a territorial animal is not the subject of this book, but it has a significant bearing on the way that managers support each other. Regardless of their apparent indifference to the idea of support decision-makers need support in three distinct and important ways (see Figure 9.1).

In its completeness this supportive environment will encourage decision-makers to take decisions willingly, and to use their knowledge, experience, and the information they receive with confidence. Of course, this does not make decision-making easier, but it does provide a degree of support that will remove or reduce decision anxiety.

The role of information

In Figure 9.1 information appears from all three directions. Some of this will be formal (part of a regular system) and some informal (hearsay, ideas, etc.). For many managers the informal information flows are used more often and with more confidence than formal information. This is particularly the case with complex decisions. In mechanical and routine decisions reliance is placed more on the formal information flows.

Information systems, then, are good and supportive for mechanical and routine decisions, and much less so for complex decision-making. However, this should not lead to any underestimation of the importance of information for decision-making.

Perfect and imperfect information

It is almost certainly true that managers will never have 'perfect information', i.e. exactly the right information at the right time to make a decision. They will have to work with 'imperfect information', i.e. some elements will be lacking, thus increasing the risk inherent in the decision. Avoiding the decision because of lack of information does not help, as the decision will almost certainly have some time boundary. The answer lies in managers knowing the degree of 'imperfection' in the information and using the information they do have to minimise the impact this will have on the decision. Using spreadsheets to look at 'what-if?' scenarios is one way of attempting to reduce the risks.

> ## The unsupported manager
>
> 'Good morning Harry, I've asked you to pop in because I want to talk about the decision to close number 3 works.'
>
> 'Yes, I thought that might be it.'
>
> 'Well, where are you up to?'
>
> 'I'm getting pretty close now, I'm just waiting for the information on the closure costs, and the latest market figures, and then I think I can wrap it up.'
>
> 'Good, let me know as soon as you decide what to do.'
>
> Harry left the office feeling even more under pressure than before. No one else seemed to want to suggest what to do, or to give him the information he wanted. He was having to chase all over the place to ferret out the simplest facts and figures.
>
> 'Hello Peter, it's Harry speaking. Can you spare some time to talk to me about the projected sales from number 3 works...? You'll send a fax, thanks, but I would like to discuss it with you.... OK, if you're that busy just send me the fax.'
>
> 'David, it's Harry. That's right, it's about number 3 works. OK, I know it's difficult, but I really would appreciate it if you could be at the meeting. I'm basing a lot of my suggestions on your cost figures.... OK, you'll do your best.'
>
> Harry finally went to see his boss.
>
> 'Well, my decision is to close number 3 works at the end of March. By then we will have...'
>
> 'Yes, yes, I'm sure you have made the right decision, you will need to think about announcing it and the implications. And remember, this is your decision, any comeback and it's on your head.'

This scenario may seem to you to be a bit extreme, but this kind of unsupported environment exists in many organisations. People fear the negative results that might arise from some decisions and distance themselves from them, but when everything turns out to be alright they all want to claim some part in the success.

> ## 9.5 My support environment
>
> Think about the environment you work in and assess the support you can count on from the three levels, i.e. above, below and alongside.

9.4 External data sources

All organisations exist in an environment from which they draw sustenance and provide some return. It is certain, therefore, that much of the data that is needed for the organisation's success will come from outside the organisation itself.

There are five main areas of external information that have to be paid close attention: markets, products, the economy, trading partners, and networks.

Markets

It is important that an organisation is aware of the changing needs of the marketplace that it serves. This information can come from industry groupings such as trade associations, or from professional companies that watch and report on market trends. Knowing what competitors are doing with market intelligence is probably one of the most important sources of strategic information.

Needless to say, such information on markets is not easy to obtain or cheap to purchase. But it should be an important external focus for those charged with managing corporate information.

Products

Every organisation provides a service or produces products for its customers. These can stay the same for many years, but they can also change constantly. Whatever the organisation is doing or making will have a life cycle, which is determined partly by customer demand and partly by technological changes. Of course, this will change at a speed determined by type of product or service.

Figure 9.2 shows the stages of the life cycle.

Figure 9.2: Product life cycle

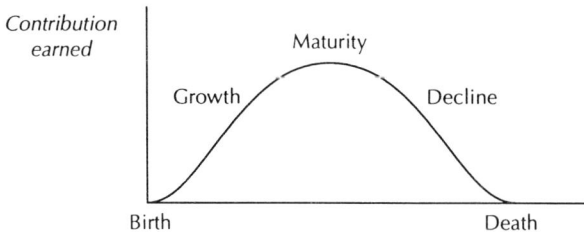

It is important to be able to produce information that plots product life cycles and to obtain information on all aspects of the product and service in terms of its stability or susceptibility to change.

The world of computers and telecommunications is one with very short product life cycles. Any organisation in this business has to keep a very careful watch on developments. This kind of information is available from special interest groups, industry associations and companies that operate market research, either on commission or speculatively for particular products.

The economy

This is an area where information can be purchased that is specific to an organisation in terms of the impact that current economic factors may have on that organisation. There are also companies that offer information services by searching the press, both trade and national, for information that might be of interest. These abstracting services can be expensive, but very useful.

The organisation's own professional advisers, in the form of banks, accountants, lawyers, etc., will provide regular reports and updates of economic indicators and their impact on the organisation.

Trading partners

The organisation, if in business, will work closely with customers, suppliers, and sub-contractors. (Employees are included here as members of the organisation.)

Information from trading partners will overlap some of the other external information, but will usually have a much more direct impact on business activities. This information should be extended as far as possible. With the increase in electronic data interchange (EDI), this open exchange of information between trading partners is essential. It might also be useful to use external agencies for information about trading partners, especially at the beginning of the relationship. Credit ratings and company searches spring readily to mind.

All these aspects of external information are important. There is little point focusing on internally generated information about what is happening if the outside world is ignored. It would be like driving a car without any windows by using the speedometer, petrol gauge and mileometer. Useful as these instruments are, little progress would be made.

Networks

The growing use of networks, such as the Internet and the World Wide Web, allows access to considerable amounts of data generated outside the boundaries of the organisation. This has the advantage of broadening the scope for gathering data relevant to decisions, and the disadvantage of adding another volume of data to be searched. However, as access methods and timing improve, and as the services offered by these networks become more easily identified, so they will need to be included as part of the information equation.

9.5 Uncertainty and risk

Uncertainty

Chapter 8 covered risk in the sense of 'information economics', and how the value of information could partly be assessed by the degree to which it reduced risk in decision-making. But there will always be an element of uncertainty in any decision.

Two things are certain: future events are unclear, and death. Everything else carries some degree of uncertainty.

This can be seen on a simple scale of 0–1, where 0 is the completely unknown and 1 is absolute certainty. This is the probability scale, and the outcome of every decision can be rated on it. You will have come across mathematical formulae which use probability analysis and decision trees as a way of helping to assess the degree of risk involved in decision-making.

In terms of information management, it is important that uncertainty is acknowledged. If it were possible to calculate the exact result of different courses of action, and if the choice were based on the highest profit, or lowest cost alternative, then there would in fact be no decision, but a simple selection of the appropriate course as indicated by the figures. But such a situation rarely occurs in the strategic area, occasionally in the operational area, and never in planning.

Risk

Risk is the measure of the degree of uncertainty, or the degree of probability of any particular outcome occurring. Providing information to deal with this depends on the following:

- Reliability of
- Information
- Systems, and
- Knowledge.

If managers receive information they can trust, and know how to use the information, then they can reduce the risk of any particular choice of action (decision). Decision-making is all about making choices and can only be done when managers receive information which helps them to evaluate a variety of possibilities. The computer is particularly helpful here, because many different scenarios can be examined through 'what-if?' facilities, rather than only the single set of chosen – and possibly biased – data they may be presented with.

But when can managers trust the information they receive? There are four factors at play here:

- *Experience* has shown managers that the information they receive has, in the past, proven its value in guiding them to making effective decisions.
- *Availability* of the information matches their needs, i.e. it is available when and where they need it.
- *Verification* of the information is possible from several sources, and past verification has proven the quality of the information.
- *Adaptation* of the system is possible to deal with changing circumstances, and this has happened in the past.

When these four factors are all met managers become comfortable with, and rely on, the information they receive. So it is little wonder that they resist changes which threaten this trusted system.

Risk management and assessment

Perhaps the key element in handling risk is to be able to determine the extent of risk involved in any particular choice or series of choices. For the inevitable deficiencies in management information you should refer back to the words of Peter Drucker, quoted on page 68.

We can't afford not to do it

A small engineering company was subcontracting a particular kind of milling operation to an outside company that had the necessary computer-controlled large-bed miller (a special machine for finishing large castings). The outside company was a competitor for some of the company's products. After some delays had occurred in the supply of the completed parts the factory manager requested the purchase of a computer-controlled large-bed miller.

The management accountant had worked out the appropriate discounted cash flow capital appraisal, which indicated a very poor return from the investment. Thus he recommended that the request should be turned down, because there were other more beneficial investments in the pipeline. At a special meeting arranged to discuss the proposal the factory manager had put his case as follows.

'We are currently producing nine ball grinders a month that produce a contribution of £110,000. To produce these machines we need to have three parts machined externally on the large-bed miller. These cost only £500 per ball grinder. If we were to machine these in-house they would cost £400, a saving of £100 per ball grinder or £900 a month. This will not produce a good return on investment, but it will protect us from the actions of our competitors, and it will ensure the continued contribution from our sales of ball grinders. Even if we only cover the cost of capital from the savings it is worth it.

'I suggest that this is an investment we can't afford not to make.'

In this scenario the factory manager was concerned about a risk different from that bothering the management accountant. The risk of losing business and being at the mercy of a competitor was more important to the factory manager than the risk of achieving a good rate of return on investment. To deal with this the factory manager had been able to assemble information from his trusted system to support his argument. The investment was approved, and subsequently the company went on to produce and sell more than twenty ball grinders a month.

9.6 Summary

- There are four main factors involved in designing appropriate information strategies: technology; systems; business needs; and people.
- Performance indicators are important in arriving at the information needs of managers.
- To be effective, managers need decision support from systems and people.
- External data sources are becoming increasingly important in the information equation.
- Risk is an inherent part of decision-making and can be reduced by appropriate access to relevant information.

10 Presentation of Information

10.1 Introduction

Traditional problems

The ability to present information effectively has always been a primary requirement for anyone whose job it is to inform management. Unfortunately it is not an activity that comes naturally or easily to the majority of people. This is particularly true of accounting information. It seems that people are locked into a straitjacket of columns and rows of figures.

Historically accountants used ruled paper on which to write the numbers that were so important for measuring performance. Gradually these manual documents were replaced by typed versions using special accounting typewriters that had extensive tabulation facilities so that the columns and rows could be maintained. Then came accounting machines that perpetuated the columns-and-rows presentation style. And, with the arrival of computers, the approach was continued. So even today, with the most sophisticated computers, accounting reports are still produced in columns and rows.

It is sometimes possible to believe that accountants are unable to think of any other possibilities. The very nature of bookkeeping requires that figures are kept in neat columns. To do otherwise would make it very difficult to carry out the essential arithmetic. The fact that computers have changed the form of bookkeeping seems to have been lost on accountants.

But computers have themselves helped to perpetuate the columns-and-rows concept. Spreadsheet packages have been designed both to cater for accounting needs and to foster the use of the computer's preference for using matrices. This preference is to make the mathematics easier to carry out, record. and present.

The importance of relevance

When people want information they usually have a specific need. If, for example, managers want the current unit production cost of a particular product, they do not want a full production cost sheet with comparisons between actual and standard presented in columns and rows. They probably want to know something like this:

Actual unit cost £18.21, which is £0.75 better than standard owing to a favourable price for raw materials

This information is relevant for the particular need. If the need is not clear then a few questions should soon identify the need. Asking managers what they are planning to use the information for is the first and most critical question. This can then be followed by more questions to ensure that the information provided is exactly right for the purpose for which it is to be used. This is the basic principle of relevance reporting.

This chapter covers the way that modern technology has helped us to rethink the ways that information, and particularly accounting information, can be stored, manipulated and presented to enable relevance reporting to replace old-fashioned methods of presenting information. Some of the ideas covered have always been possible with a little imagination; others have become possible because of the developments in information technology.

Performance

Feedback is vitally important to successful decision-making. In the middle of battle generals need information about the disposition of troops, movements of the enemy, supply lines, ammunition, and myriad detailed logistical facts and figures. A constant flow of up-to-date information is needed. This regular flow of information feeds decision-making about current operations, and also influences decisions about future activities.

The value of information is related to its usefulness at both strategic and tactical levels. So it follows that the first vital step for those responsible for corporate information is to establish exactly what the strategic and tactical needs are. For most organisations this will fall into three or four key activity areas. Establishing what these are, and concentrating investment and effort in these areas, can pay handsome dividends.

Presentation

Good presentation of information is critical for its effective use. To have value, information must be useful. To be useful, information must be relevant, simple, clear, concise, current and accurate. These are the key factors that will be dealt with fully later in this chapter. It is, however, first worth emphasising the critical importance of presentation.

Cost of lost production

Some years ago, while working for an engineering company, TJ attempted to introduce a preventive maintenance system. For several months the factory cost report showed rising maintenance costs and, in spite of his protests, the system was abandoned. Over the next three months, maintenance costs fell and the management felt pleased. TJ decided to present a special report on maintenance to support his arguments for a preventive system. The chart shown below, displaying clearly the variation of lost production hours with maintenance costs, was so effective that preventive maintenance was reintroduced.

Figure 10.1: Preventive maintenance

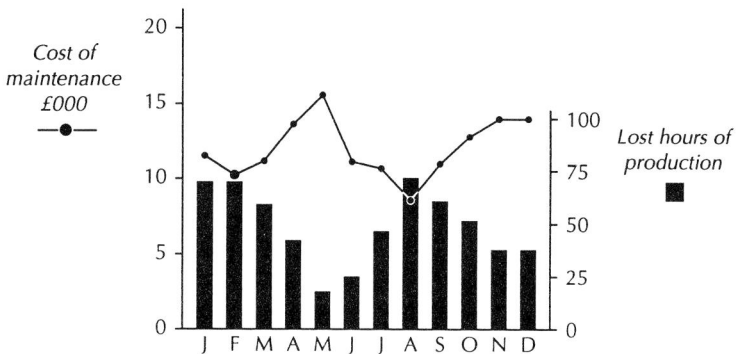

There are many pitfalls to avoid when presenting information, all of which in some way conflict with the key factors: relevance, simplicity, clarity, conciseness, currency and accuracy. Perhaps the four worst pitfalls are:

- too much;
- too detailed;
- too often; and
- too precise.

These pitfalls will all be covered later, but perhaps the above example will serve to show how all of these have been avoided. so that the message is effective, i.e. it is both received and understood.

10.2 Relevance reporting

Information is relevant when it provides exactly what is sought about a particular activity or event. Relevance reporting is the provision of information about specified activities and events in accordance with the current needs of individual managers. This calls for flexibility in the process of presenting information. It also implies that those responsible for presenting information will endeavour to relate information to the current needs of individual managers.

There are six essential steps in relevance reporting:

LIVERPOOL JOHN MOORES UNIVERSITY
LEARNING SERVICES

- establishing current information needs;
- prioritising and targeting needs;
- extracting relevant information;
- choosing the presentation format;
- assessing usefulness; and
- adapting relevance reports.

All of these steps sound fairly obvious, yet are all too frequently ignored. Some pointers for each step follow.

Establishing current needs

This involves a *continuing* dialogue to establish what areas of concern individual managers may have, and to discuss with them the type of information that will help. As it is likely that there will be many concerns, these need to be discussed in regard to both the value and the cost of the information. For example, a production manager might be concerned about overall unit costs, about material wastage, about lost production time, about one particular large order, about the output of a particular machine, and about efficiency of the internal transport system. This list of needs will change (and hence the need for continuing dialogue), but for the moment these are the areas of concern. If information is provided which does not help in these areas, it is unlikely to get the manager's attention.

Prioritising and targeting needs

In the above example, if the manager's needs are prioritised, it may emerge that the critical area, in the manager's opinion, is the internal transport system. This then is targeted for a relevance report, as may be all the other needs in a descending order of importance as agreed with the manager.

Extracting relevant information

This is the process where the information providers have to make use of the information systems. including the management accounting system, to find and extract the relevant information. Note that this task of extracting information should *not* become a burden to managers. Unfortunately this important point is often overlooked, and managers are frequently presented with voluminous, detailed reports from which they have to try to glean the information they need. This is not only a lazy approach; it is also inefficient and time-wasting.

Choosing a relevant presentation format

There are many ways in which information can be presented, and it is the job of information providers to agree with managers the way(s) in which they want to receive information. Different people have different preferences, and it is important to recognise what these are and then, as far as is possible, to cater for them.

For example. there is little point in presenting information graphically if the intended recipients prefer text and numbers. Similarly. if the recipients find it useful to get information in a columns-and-rows format, then this is how it should be provided. Later in this chapter the primary media of presentation are discussed further.

Assessing usefulness

It is unlikely that managers will know how useful the information is until *after* they have received and used it. In relevance reporting it is important for information providers to get feedback on five main points:

- timeliness;
- content;
- format;
- accuracy; and
- style.

It is helpful to provide managers with a duplicate copy of the report to be returned to the provider with a simple feedback statement, a template for which is shown in Figure 10.2. If the report to which it relates is screen-based then the statement can be attached to a screen print or in some other way referenced to the particular screen.

Figure 10.2: Template for simple feedback system

	Excellent	Good	OK	Unhelpful	Poor
Timeliness					
Content					
Format					
Accuracy					
Style					

Please tick the appropriate box. If you would like to make any suggestions for improvement, please do so on the reverse of this sheet.

Such a feedback statement could be followed up, and can hence help to lead to improvements in the effectiveness of the relevance reporting system.

Adapting relevance reports

Once feedback has been received, changes in the reporting can be discussed and agreed. This process will probably happen many times and may become a continuing feature of the relevance reporting system. Fortunately, modern information technology makes it possible constantly to change content and format without any major difficulties and/or cost.

Regular, all-encompassing reports presented in the same way month after month are not only boring and mainly irrelevant to specific needs, but also inefficient, time wasting and costly.

If routine reports are not used then they have no value. The process used to collect, record, manipulate and store data has a value that is quite separate from the value of the information generated from it. Hence the primary value of corporate databases rests in the availability of the data, if and when it is needed. The primary value of information however, rests in its relevance to specific decisions.

10.3 Numerical versus textual presentation

A number is a symbol representing quantity. It is a symbol that can be used to manipulate data about quantities and, as such, is an extremely valuable concept. It is the basis of accounting and, to a large extent, the basis of computing. There is little doubt that to present numerical information in a textual form would be both time-consuming and confusing. Presentation of information solely in a numerical form can, however, be difficult to read and may also lead to confusion. This topic of presentation is worth pursuing in greater depth as, however good the quality of information, it can be rendered worthless by poor presentation.

The need for a balanced approach

What is needed is a balanced approach. Unfortunately the nature of computer-based information systems has not made this an easy prospect, but things are changing as the importance of good presentation has been increasingly recognised.

Earlier in this chapter we noted the widespread use of the columns and rows format for presenting numerical data. This is perhaps the most common way of presenting numerical data, but it is also the most difficult to read and use. A simple example of this is shown in Figure 10.3. The presentation itself is simple and clear, with only the significant numbers being shown. If, however, the report had been in £s instead of £000s it would have been almost unreadable. But, even in its present form, it is unclear what it is intended to show. How can the reader's attention be directed to relevant information? Even when the relevant information can be spotted there is no explanation attaching to it.

Contrast this columns-and-rows presentation with the report shown in Figure 10.4. Admittedly, for those accustomed to reading columns and rows of numbers the alternative text style might not be an advantage, but for busy managers it can be a considerable improvement. If this information is presented on-line with the option for the manager to access the detailed statement then we would have the best of both worlds.

Figure 10.3: The columns-and-rows approach

PRODUCTION COST REPORT: JUNE (All figures, £000)

Last Month			Machine shop	This month			Year to date		
ACT	BUD	VAR		ACT	BUD	VAR	ACT	BUD	VAR
272	240	(32)	Direct labour	231	220	(11)	1220	1150	(70)
350	360	10	Direct materials	311	300	(11)	1800	1900	100
40	36	(4)	Direct expenses	31	30	(1)	190	180	(10)
662	636	(26)	Total direct	573	550	(23)	3210	3230	20
23	20	(3)	Maintenance	21	20	(1)	130	120	(10)
7	6	(1)	Oils and greases	5	6	1	33	36	2
2	5	3	Cleaning	7	9	2	30	40	10
8	12	4	Internal transport	11	13	2	71	70	(1)
12	10	(2)	Cranes	13	10	(3)	72	60	(12)
6	8	2	Consumables	9	12	3	45	60	15
20	23	3	Supervision	21	23	2	130	138	8
4	5	1	Tool setting	11	5	(6)	52	30	(22)
5	6	1	Tool repairs	10	6	(4)	56	36	(20)
6	6	–	Lighting	6	6	-	36	36	–
21	20	(1)	Energy	24	20	(4)	140	120	(20)
16	14	(2)	Administration	15	14	(1)	90	84	(6)
130	135	5	Total indirect	153	144	(9)	885	830	(55)
792	771	(21)	Total machine shop	726	694	(32)	4095	4060	(35)

Figure 10.4: Alternative production cost report

Owing to an increase in throughput of 8% for the second month running the direct costs were (23,000) above budget. This brings the year-to-date figure very close to budget with the adverse direct labour variance of (70,000) being more than offset by the favourable direct material variance of 100,000.

The year to date overspend on indirect costs of (55,000) is mainly due to tool setting (22,000) and tool repairs (20,000), as well as an overspend of (20,000) on energy. The energy overspend can be attributed to the increased throughput, as can part of the tool costs overspend. However, the consistent high overspend on tool setting and repairs is worrying. Fortunately the overspends are partly offset by underspending on cleaning and consumables, though the current untidy state of the factory could mean that we have been too diligent in curtailing these costs.

The overall cost performance is close to budget and with the increase in throughput the results for the month and the year to date are satisfactory.

PRODUCTION COST SUMMARY REPORT: JUNE (All figures, £000)

Last Month			Machine shop	This month			Year to date		
ACT	BUD	VAR		ACT	BUD	VAR	ACT	BUD	VAR
662	636	(26)	Total direct	573	550	(23)	3210	3230	20
130	135	5	Total indirect	153	144	(9)	885	830	(55)
792	771	(21)	Total machine shop	726	694	(32)	4095	4060	(35)

The presentation of numerical data can also be made pictorially rather than in columns and rows, and with current computer capabilities this can be effected quite easily. Software is now generally available that will convert spreadsheet data into a choice of pictorial forms at the press of a button. These may still need to be accompanied with text, however, and this may be more difficult.

Perhaps the most powerful way to present numerical information is with a combination of numbers, text and pictures. This is perfectly possible with modern computer facilities. What is needed is essentially a combination of a spreadsheet, a graphics facility and a word processor. If a calculator and a database facility for storage are also added then we have a powerful information presentation system. Such systems are available and are generally referred to as executive information systems (EIS).

When presenting numerical information, no matter how it is done, it is important to pay careful attention to three primary criteria: content, accuracy and significance.

Content

It is very easy to misunderstand the information needs that managers express, and thus to include information that is not required or to exclude that which is, and by doing so to cause confusion.

Wheels within wheels

The transport manager asked for a report on repair costs for individual vehicles in a fleet of 600. The data was collected and a report was produced which was subdivided into categories of vehicles by regions. It was a sizable task to prepare the report. When he finally received it, the manager was shocked by the scale of the repair costs, which were much higher than expected. A more detailed examination was then started when the manager discovered that the figures included services, oil and tyres: these were not considered to be repair costs. The report therefore had to be recompiled, and the manager was eventually able to recover and complete the exercise of comparing the repair costs of different types of vehicles.

Accuracy

Most managers would say that the numerical data included in reports should be both complete and correct. But this should actually mean that it is sufficiently complete, and sufficiently correct, for the purpose for which the information is needed. With modern statistical facilities it is rarely necessary to have 100 per cent of the data to 100 per cent correctness, even if this were possible. What is necessary is that enough data is available to the acceptable degree of error. The amount of data collected and the margin of error may well depend upon the speed with which the information is required.

In order to establish the desired accuracy the purpose for which the information is needed must be known. Attention must be paid to the quality of the data being collected, especially when this data is entered into a computer and becomes part of an 'accurate' data processing system.

What a clanger

TJ liked to tell the story of the sophisticated, computer-based material control system that depended on a closing stock figure to calculate material usage. The stock figure was arrived at by banging the side of an enclosed silo with a large spanner and judging the volume of the contents by the resulting sound!

Significance

There is often a desire to present all the information, even when a great deal of it is insignificant. When numerical data is presented in columns and rows the numbers should be limited to four or five digits across the columns. This may mean presenting the information in hundreds, thousands, tens of thousands, hundreds of thousands, or millions. This both makes the information easier to read, and emphasises the key figures. Figure 10.5. shows an extract of the report contained in Figure 10.3. Though the example is only a small part of a report it is obvious how much more difficult it is to read. It is also obvious how the additional numbers add no value whatsoever to the information.

Figure 10.5: Report extract

Machine shop	This month			Year to date		
	ACT	BUD	VAR	ACT	BUD	VAR
Direct labour	231,238	220,486	(10,752)	1,220,145	1,150,398	(69,747)
Direct materials	331,321	299,895	(11,426)	1,800,376	1,900,471	100,095
Direct expenses	31,456	30,112	(1,344)	189,973	180,176	(9,797)
Total direct	574,015	550,493	(23,552)	3,210,494	3,210,494	20,551

No matter how numerical information is presented, i.e. whether on paper or on the computer screen, the principles of good presentation still apply. Information technology offers many advantages and allows considerable flexibility, but it must be used intelligently, and with flair and imagination.

10.4 Presentation styles

There are five principal styles of presentation of information which can be termed illustratively:

- military;
- focus;
- pinpoint;
- fishing; and
- haystack.

These styles offer a variety of options which should suit most people depending upon what they want.

The military style

This style is epitomised by the columns-and-rows approach discussed earlier. Everything is neat and tidy and the numbers are in the exact position determined by their size and significance. The picture is one of order and discipline. Rank after rank of numbers march across the page, and readers find it hard to distinguish individual numbers from the massed ranks passing in front of their eyes. The order and neatness can give a false impression of the underlying content and value of the information. Who would dare to question such a well-formed and disciplined set of numbers'?

The focus style

Here the emphasis is different: start with a block of numbers in a military formation,, but then focus on individual or blocks of numbers which have a particular relevance. This can be effected in several ways. For example, the focus can be introduced by text referring to the context from which the information has been extracted. Alternatively, the full military presentation can be shown, and then the focus, or a picture shown with the focus expanding a part of it. The example in Figure 10.6. uses the second approach, where the full military style report is shown with the focus being indicated both diagrammatically and with explanatory text.

The pinpoint style

This is similar to the focus style except that the wider context is not considered. The information needed is pinpointed by the manager involved and a report is prepared specifically dealing with the desired content. An example is shown in Figure 10.7.

Figure 10.6: Example of the focus style

PRODUCTION COST REPORT: JUNE (All figures, £000)										
Last Month			Machine shop	This month			Year to date			
ACT	BUD	VAR		ACT	BUD	VAR	ACT	BUD	VAR	
272	240	(32)	Direct labour	231	220	(11)	1220	1150	(70)	
350	360	10	Direct materials	311	300	(11)	1800	1900	100	
40	36	(4)	Direct expenses	31	30	(1)	190	180	(10)	
662	636	(26)	Total direct	573	550	(23)	3210	3230	20	
23	20	(3)	Maintenance	21	20	(1)	130	120	(10)	
7	6	(1)	Oils and greases	5	6	1	33	36	2	
2	5	3	Cleaning	7	9	2	30	40	10	
8	12	4	Internal transport	11	13	2	71	70	(1)	
12	10	(2)	Cranes	13	10	(3)	72	60	(12)	
6	8	2	Consumables	9	12	3	45	60	15	
20	23	3	Supervision	21	23	2	130	138	8	
4	5	1	Tool setting	11	5	(6)	52	30	(22)	
5	6	1	Tool repairs	10	6	(4)	56	36	(20)	
6	6	–	Lighting	6	6	-	36	36	–	
21	20	(1)	Energy	24	20	(4)	140	120	(20)	
16	14	(2)	Administration	15	14	(1)	90	84	(6)	
130	135	5	Total indirect	153	144	(9)	885	830	(55)	
792	771	(21)	Total machine shop	726	694	(32)	4095	4060	(35)	

Tool setting
The significant overspend on tool setting has four main reasons:
* the constant changes on the new comuterised lathes;
* the learning curve for the fitters;
* the high faiure of tools from our new supplier;
* the increased throughput.

Tool repairs
The overspend on tool repairs has three reasons:
* the high failure of tools from our new supplier;
* incorrect use of tools on the new computerised lathes;
* increased cost of materials, particularly industrial diamonds and titanium.

Figure 10.7: Example of the pinpoint style

Report on overspend on tool setting and tool repairs

Tool setting

The overspend for the year to date on tool setting is £21,922. This is made up as follows;

Labour costs	11,895	extended overtime particularly on new lathes
Supervision	4,321	assistance and training on new lathes.
Training	3,595	new lathes
Consumables	2,111	additional work: extra throughput and new lathes
Total	21,922	

Tool repairs

The overspend for the year to date on tool repairs is £20,200. This is made up as follows;

Materials costs	9,750	increased prices for diamonds and titanium
Labour costs	4,850	overtime to repair tools for new lathes
Scrapped tools	4,300	excess breakages on tools from new supplier
Supervision	1,300	extra design work and overtime.
Total	20,200	

A more detailed breakdown of the labour cost overspend on tool setting and the material cost overspend on tool repairs can be supplied if needed.

The fishing style

This style is often used when people are unclear about what they want to know. It is rather like going out to collect data to see what turns up. It involves presenting information in such a way as to draw attention to things which seem interesting, and then leaving it to the managers to spot the fish swimming in a sea of information.

The main technique for presenting information in a fishing style is to use a basic military style, and then to highlight certain information. Ways of highlighting are: underlining, asterisks, boxes and circles on printed reports; and flashing, reverse video, underlining, colours and high intensity on screen-based reports.

This style is sometimes adopted because information providers are nervous about actually focusing on or pinpointing the information.

The haystack style

This is the style used by many accountants. It is based on the idea that the more information, the better. Every possible piece of information is given. Reports run to many pages of detailed information. There are summaries supported by ever-increasing levels of detail, and different varieties of analysis. It is usually necessary to train new managers in the reading of the reports, which come out with monotonous regularity and always in the same format. With these reports managers are challenged to find 'the needle of pertinent fact in a haystack of irrelevance' – hardly a helpful approach.

Fortunately the use of EIS and other database facilities such as report writers are helping to eliminate haystack reports.

All the styles mentioned above are evident in both printed and screen-based versions. The very nature of the use of screens can provide a more selective approach to accessing and reporting information. So perhaps much more use of the focus and pinpoint styles of reporting will be seen in future.

10.5 Presentation media

The medium chosen for presenting information will depend on the circumstances and on the preference of individuals. No matter which medium is chosen, the key factors of relevance, simplicity, clarity, conciseness, currency and accuracy still apply. No matter how sophisticated the possibilities, these key factors should always be uppermost in the minds of the presenters of information. Modern computer software and equipment provide a bewildering array of possibilities, from palettes of hundreds of colours to text in many different typefaces and sizes. Resisting the temptation to dabble is very hard.

There is a certain artistic skill in good layout, and it is a skill in very short supply. People try to use far too many colours and typefaces and end up with a confusing mess. They have obviously forgotten the key factors of simplicity and clarity.

The media used for most presentations appeal to the senses of sight and hearing. 'Sight' covers the written word as well as pictures, so can be split into 'reading' and 'seeing'.

Reading

Reading is performed both from paper and from computer screens. It is easier to read from paper than the screen, and this seems to be the preferred approach. Even when information is presented on-screen, many people print it out and then study it. Regardless of whether the information is presented on paper or screen it should:

- be laid out with plenty of space;
- flow from left to right and from top to bottom;
- use upper and lower case, except for headings;
- use no more than four colours, including black and white.

Presenting information to be read on paper means using some form of printing and/or copying from an original. Modern laser printers ensure that information being printed from computer files is crisp and clear. The days of poor-quality dot-matrix printers have all but disappeared, and with the growth of desktop publishing facilities there is no longer any excuse for poorly produced printed reports.

Screen-based presentation offers considerable scope, especially given facilities such as hypertext for accessing more information by focusing on key data on the screen and then dropping down several levels of detail. Windows also provide further detail from a particular field on the screen. These facilities have to be used with care otherwise they can be more confusing than helpful. The basic principles of presenting text and numbers should always be considered regardless of the facility being used. A screen is like a printed page. It may be scrolled up and down, and from side to side, but it should still be seen as a page.

Electronic mail (e-mail) is gradually moving a lot of information from paper to screen. so eventually it is probable that people will get used to the idea of using screens without a printed version of the information.

Seeing

'Seeing' can he distinguished from 'reading' in terms of the use of graphics and pictures instead of words. With modern technology it is possible to provide both printed and screen-based pictures and graphs of a very high quality. This means that there is likely to be a move towards the use of this form of presentation. All the key factors of presentation must be considered, but emphasis should be on simplicity, clarity and accuracy. There is a very common and bad practice, widely used when presenting information graphically, and that is to show the information using inaccurate scales. The bar charts in Figure 10.8 show an example of the effect of this. Chart (a) appears to show a much greater rise and fall than chart (b). This is because the scale used does not start at zero. This may well be constructed deliberately in order to deceive.

Figure 10.8: Contrasting bar charts

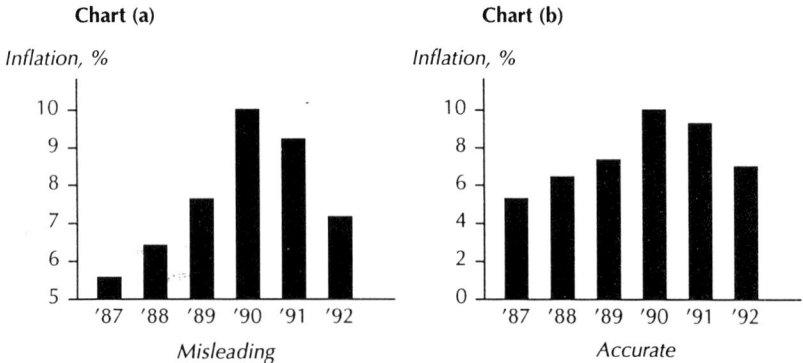

Whenever graphics are used in a representative way, care should be taken to avoid deceiving the audience. The information should be presented accurately and be mathematically correct. If necessary, numbers should be superimposed on the graphs, particularly on pie diagrams. Video and video text are ways of presenting information on the screen. With video we also have the possibility of movement and sound, making it a very powerful presentation medium. Very effective management reports can be produced using slides and a recording from a script, with a video produced from the tape slide format. The extra power of the spoken word adds to the pictures, and gives one of the best combined presentation media.

Hearing

A considerable amount of information is presented using the spoken word. This can be over the telephone, via tapes, to accompany pictures (video), voice mail, face-to-face conversations, lectures and meetings. Unfortunately most people are rather poor listeners, which makes the effective use of this medium quite difficult. Add to this the problem of constructing a message which is simple, clear, concise, accurate and relevant to the listener, and it is easy to see why the spoken medium is so ineffective.

Our sense of hearing is quite complex. Hearing can be tuned to pick up sounds amid a background of loud noise. This is the process of listening. Paying attention in this way gives the chance to 'hear' and understand the message.

Presenting information via the spoken word is perhaps the most widely used and yet least effective means of presentation.. Messages are frequently misunderstood; people say things they do not mean, and mean things they do not say. And yet when it is done properly, and particularly if it is done in conjunction with some visual medium, it can be very effective.

If the spoken word is the chosen medium there are three steps to follow to make it work:

- Construct the message carefully before speaking, stating clearly what the listener is required to understand.
- Break the message down into several simple, clear points using short sentences and simple well-known words.
- Check after each point that the listener has received and understood the message.

It is often a good idea to write down what you want to say as if you were writing a letter to the other person.

Using the spoken word is becoming an ever more widely used method of giving information. Computer-based voice systems are on the increase, and services such as voice mail, where spoken messages can be left, are increasingly being used.

All the media available for presentation of information have their advantages and disadvantages, and people receiving information have their preferences. It is always advisable to try to establish which is the preferred, and therefore the most effective, way of informing individual managers. If managers are to respond well to the information with which they are presented, then – and it seems obvious to say it – they should be given it in a form in which they like to receive it.

10.6 Presentation pitfalls

There are many pitfalls in the effective presentation of information. These are mostly concerned with ignoring the key factors: relevance, simplicity, clarity, conciseness, currency and accuracy. Even when these factors are observed, however, it is still possible to trip over the matchstick of good intentions. Six of the principal pitfalls are described in the following sections.

The bear trap

Hidden deep in the forest of information, out of sight beneath a superficial cover of seemingly innocent data, lies a deep hole into which managers are likely to fall if they do not have their wits about them. Bear traps can be produced deliberately, but most of the time they are created accidentally. They occur mainly when the level of information is too high for the purpose for which it is required. This may be through lack of time, laziness, or the lack of a suitable level of data collection.

Whatever the cause, the information is not provided at a sufficiently detailed level.

There is a bear trap in the information on machine shop costs in Figure 10.3. The information shows an underspend on direct materials. On the surface this seems alright, even though we know that throughput has increased. Looking a little more closely would reveal that the underspend is due to the purchase of a supply of mild steel at considerably less than the usual price, and below the normal specified quality. There was also some extra scrap, and quite a lot of rework, which partly explains the overspend on direct labour. There is also the possibility of problems of product failure and the associated costs. Altogether this is quite a sizeable bear trap.

Bear traps are avoided by coming down to the forest floor and searching carefully through the undergrowth.

The creaky branch

Imagine the organization as a tree, with the trunk as the core of the business branching out into all the detailed activities. In this scenario, the information system is like the sap that feeds all these activities with the nourishment they need to stay alive and active.

Sometimes, if there is a problem with the way information is presented, it can cut the flow to a particular branch, which then begins to creak. It is not difficult for this to happen.

In our example company there is a creaky branch, and this is the stores activity serving the factory. There is a stores system and there is plenty of information about stock levels and issues and receipts. There is, however, very little information about the efficiency of the stores operation. Information such as the following is unavailable:

- cost per order;
- cost per requisition;
- cost of scrap;
- obsolete stock;
- stock-outs;
- delays waiting for materials;
- wastage;
- price trends;
- range of goods in stock, leading to variety reduction;
- space utilisation.

True, this information may not have been asked for by the stores controller, but then this is part of the proactive service of information providers, or at least it should be. In the example the stores function has become a very creaky branch indeed.

Creaky branches can be avoided by constantly looking at the organisation tree and examining how all the branches can be kept healthy by being fed with good nourishing information.

The truth trap

Someone said: 'The components had to be scrapped.' The truth of the matter was as follows. The machine operator said the tool settings were wrong. The tool-setter said the program on the computerised lathe had a bug. The lathe manufacturer said the tools were set incorrectly. The section leader said it was because of the low-quality materials being used.

> There are many kinds of eyes, therefore there must be many kinds of truths, and consequently there can be no truth . *Montaigne*

In presenting information there is no truth. There are facts and opinions. Presenters fall into the truth trap when they make statements which sound like truth, but which are actually either facts or opinions. In the example in Figure 10.4 there is a statement that appears as a truth, but which is actually an opinion. It is in the report where the presenter states 'though the current untidy state of the factory'. This is a truth trap and will almost certainly generate a resistant and defensive attitude from the factory manager.

Truth traps can be avoided by remembering that facts are just that, and that opinions must be expressed as opinions. Comments such as 'I think', 'I believe', or 'in my opinion' should always precede opinions.

The quickie

Some managers request 'urgent' information about specific situations. This is perfectly reasonable. Information providers often react with a report that falls into the category of a 'quickie'. This is a report which pays more attention to the speed of presentation than the quality of the content.

Information must be relevant, current and accurate. The balance between currency and accuracy is such that the more accuracy that is wanted, the longer it will take, and vice versa. Although 'fast' does not always mean 'inaccurate', there is a distinct possibility that if speed becomes critical then more accuracy must be sacrificed.

The important element of providing speedy information and avoiding the quickie is always to express the likely degree of accuracy so that the user can use the information with a full understanding of its suitability for its purpose.

The pretty picture trap

There is a common belief that if something looks good it must be good. People also believe that if the price is high so is the quality. Both are self-evident nonsense, but still people believe them to be true. Good-looking reports do not necessarily contain good-quality information. How often does one hear managers comment that the information must be correct as it came from a computer? Many people are seduced by pretty pictures and good-looking things.

There is no doubt that well-presented information can carry a higher degree of credibility than a scruffy-looking document, but is the content really better? Dressing up inadequate information does not make it adequate, but it can make it seem to be. This is the pretty picture trap. By all means we should present information in the best way possible within reasonable cost limits, but we should not concentrate on appearance to the detriment of the quality of the information.

There are many examples of the pretty picture trap, particularly for corporate reports and for information for employees. But with desktop publishing facilities there is even more chance of falling into the trap for routine management reports.

The pretty picture trap can be avoided by observing the following rules.

- Make sure that the improved quality of the presentation adds to the usefulness of the information. If it doesn't, then don't do it.
- Make sure that pictures, graphs, colours etc. add impact and increase the usefulness of the information. If they don't, then don't use them.
- If the higher-quality presentation improves the simplicity and clarity of the information, without reducing currency and accuracy, then do it.

The full bucket

Consider the following quotation, which was used on page 65:

> It is quite possible for management to collect more information than it can use to advantage, or which is more costly, or hinders production more than the information is worth. This is a real danger that has to be guarded against continuously, for routine that serves a valuable purpose when initiated may cease to be useful by some later change of conditions.   (*Elbourne*, 1914)

This is the full bucket. Even when the bucket is full an attempt is made to cram more in and, in the process, some is lost. Not only is the full bucket a heavy burden to carry, but much information is lost through spillage. So what is to be done? Get a bigger bucket!

Saving our forests

TJ carried out a survey of the usefulness of 37 monthly reports from the information centre (computer department). The reports added up to some 2,350 pages. The outcome of the survey was as follows:

- seven reports were no longer used by anyone;
- eleven reports were filed without being referred to;
- fifteen reports were used to some extent, but improvements were suggested for all of them, usually for them to be simplified;
- two reports were used extensively, but needed reorganising and summarising;
- two reports were printed but not sent to anyone.

The result of the survey was that the overall number of reports was reduced to eighteen, most of which were shorter. Several of the new reports were exception reports focusing on specific customers, products etc. The total number of pages was reduced to 650. A procedure was also established for a continuous review of all reports.

10.7 Summary

- The effective presentation of information combines three primary skills. The first is the ability to discover the information that is needed for effective decision-making. The second is the understanding of the data flows of the particular business. The third is the artistic imagination and flair associated with good form and layout.
- No matter how hard we try we are never going to be able to provide all the information that managers need.
- Our insatiable desire for information is driven by several needs. The first is the self-preservation against enemies. In the commercial arena, corporate survival is dependent upon information about competitors, markets, new products, government policy and so on. The second need for information is in measuring the degree of risk involved in a proposed course of action. The third is to measure and report performance.
- Information is a vital resource, but improving the quality and quantity will only create value if it is used effectively.
- Good presentation of information is critical for its effective use. To be useful, information must be relevant, simple, clear, concise, current and accurate.
- Relevance reporting is the provision of information about specified activities and events in accordance with the current needs of individual managers.

There are six essential steps in relevance reporting:

(a) establishing current information needs;
(b) prioritising and targeting needs;
(c) extracting relevant information;
(d) choosing the presentation format;

    (e) assessing usefulness; and

    (f) adapting relevance reports.

- Columns and rows are perhaps the most common way of presenting numerical data, but they are also among the most difficult to read and use. Perhaps the most powerful way to present numerical information is with a combination of numbers, text and pictures. When presenting numerical information, no matter how it is done, it is important to pay careful attention to three primary criteria, namely content, accuracy and significance.

- The five styles of presentation of information are:

    (a) the military style;

    (b) the focus style;

    (c) the pin-point style;

    (d) the fishing style; and

    (e) the haystack style.

- The medium chosen for presenting information will depend upon the circumstances and on the preference of individuals. No matter which medium is chosen, or how sophisticated it is, the key factors of relevance, simplicity, clarity, conciseness, currency and accuracy should always be uppermost in the minds of the presenters of information.

- Modern laser printers ensure that the information being printed from computer files is crisp and clear. The days of poor quality dot matrix printers have all but disappeared, and with the growth of desktop publishing facilities there is no longer any excuse for poorly produced printed reports.

- Presenting information via the spoken word is perhaps the most widely used and yet least effective means of presentation. Messages are frequently misunderstood; people say things they do not mean, and mean things they do not say. And yet when it is done properly, and particularly if it is done in conjunction with some visual medium, it can be very effective.

- The six main pitfalls to good presentation are:

    (a) the bear trap;

    (b) the creaky branch;

    (c) the truth trap;

    (d) the quickie;

    (e) the pretty picture trap; and

    (f) the full bucket.

11 Financial Models and Sensitivity Analysis

A model is a representation of reality. Whether the model is a physical, three-dimensional model – such as an airframe for testing in a wind tunnel – or an abstract symbolic model using mathematics to define it, it is nevertheless only a model.

Financial models are a symbolic representation of a business, or part of a business. They are, by their very nature, probabilistic: they are neither true nor false in their predictions.

Financial models are constructed by a process of abstracting from reality and converting attributes and relationships into symbols – the symbols of mathematics. Each model consists of a number of attributes each of which relates to the others in some way. These relationships are the 'rules' of the model. When data is fed to the model they are manipulated according to the rules. Both data and rules can be changed so that the model reflects the real world as nearly as possible.

With modern spreadsheet packages very sophisticated models can be built with many layers of detail and aggregation. Databases and graphics facilities can be linked to the spreadsheet and the results can be very effective. Of course, the true value of a financial model is not how good the results look, but how closely they represent the real world that the model is supposed to replicate.

There are many areas where financial models can be valuable. The following are some of the more common ones:

Budgets	Ratio analysis	Probability analysis
Capex	Standard costing	Product portfolios
Cash flows	Decision trees	Market analysis

Financial models have to be created from an in-depth knowledge of the business they are to represent. They can be improved with experience and/or as the real world changes. However, whatever efforts are made to make the model as close a representation as possible, it will only ever be a model. This simple fact is often forgotten and the predictions of models are treated as if they are the truth.

In building financial models there are four critical aspects to which close attention has to be paid. These are:

- the framework;
- the data;
- the calculations; and
- the presentation of information.

11.1 The framework

The easiest way to look at the framework of the model is to follow the accounting approach of columns and rows, As this is the same approach adopted by all spreadsheets it seems appropriate to use it here. Figure 11.1 depicts a very simple framework.

Figure 11.1: A framework for a model

Item	Jan	Feb	Mar	3-mth total
Sales income				
Costs:				
Labour				
Materials				
Energy				
Direct costs				
Contribution				
Indirect costs				
Net profit				
% of sales				

Perhaps the easiest way to design the framework of the model is to produce a paper-based version, such as the above, and then convert it into the symbolic representation required by the computer. In Figure 11.1 the columns and rows to be defined can be clearly seen. The attributes of the data and the relationships between the elements of the model can also be seen.

11.2 The data

The independent variables, the dependent variables and the rules (calculations) for this simple model can now be defined.

- *Independent variables*:
    Sales income Jan/Feb/Mar
    Labour costs Jan/Feb/Mar
    Material costs Jan/Feb/Mar
    Energy costs Jan/Feb/Mar
    Indirect costs Jan/Feb/Mar
- Dependent variables:
    3-mth total
    Direct costs
    Contribution
    Net profit
    % of sales

Every element (cell) on the framework (matrix) has now been identified. Data has to be input to the model for all the independent variables, and calculations defined for all the dependent variables in the sequence they should be carried out.

11.3 The calculations

The calculations (rules) for the model are a very important aspect of the way the model functions and have to be expressed with great care and precision. The following are the rules for the simple model.

Direct costs:	Sum of labour costs/material costs/energy costs
Contribution:	Sales income – direct costs
Net profit:	Contribution – indirect costs
3-mth total:	Sum of Jan/Feb/Mar
% of sales:	(Net profit ÷ Sales income) × 100, calculated for Jan/Feb/Mar/3-mth total

The particular way of expressing the rules to the computer depends on the particular package being used, but the main notation differences are '/' instead of '÷' , and '*' instead of '×'. I have used the usual mathematical notation.

Most financial modelling packages (spreadsheets) provide standard facilities for trying different combinations of data ('what-if?' exercises). For example, this simple model could be used to indicate what the effect would be of an increase in sales of 4 per cent with an increase of material costs of 3 per cent and an increase in energy costs of 2 per cent. This requirement could be fed into the model, which would present a report containing the new information. The facilities provided by the modelling package are extensive and allow easy manipulation of the basic data.

11.4 The presentation of information

Because the framework has been produced in columns and rows it does not mean that the information has to be presented in this way. Modern spreadsheets offer a variety of ways in which the information can be presented. This includes selecting data elements, producing graphics, including text, and linking to other systems such as word processing and desktop publishing.

11.5 Sensitivity analysis

Once the financial model has been created and tested as a reasonable representation of reality it can be used to test the predicted outcomes of a wide range of possibilities.

It is also possible to use the 'probability analysis' features of spreadsheets to attach measures of likely outcome to data so producing predictions of the most likely result of the interplay of all the probabilities included. In this way financial models can help management to explore the likely outcomes of varying strategies.

When using financial models in this way it is important to be aware of the 'sensitivity' of some of the 'key' variables to changes in the base data. With experience models can help management to gain a heightened awareness of those aspects of the business which can have the greatest effect on the bottom line.

11.6 Disadvantages and advantages of financial models

Models may look like the real thing – but they are not. Nevertheless, people compare actual results with the budget, as if the actual is wrong and the budget is right – when, of course, the opposite is true. What is of interest in such situations is the way in which reality differed from what was expected.

The disadvantages of financial models all stem from their misuse.

- There is a danger of oversimplification. The model builder may leave out crucial factors because of ignorance or expediency.
- Symbolic language, although useful, is limited and not all relationships can be expressed mathematically.
- Model builders can become so enamoured of their models that they begin to believe they are more accurate than reality.
- Models produce only predictions of outcomes.
- Models are, of course, never (or extremely rarely) absolutely right, and in some peoples' minds must therefore always be wrong.

In spite of the limitations of financial models they do have advantages:

- They provide a framework for examining problems. Though they may not always lead to solutions they can highlight gaps in information.
- The process of building the model contributes significantly to a better understanding of the problem
- They allow manipulation of both the rules and the data to test a wide variety of possible outcomes.
- They are easier and less expensive than carrying out a full-scale or even a pilot exercise saving both effort and money.

11.7 Summary

Financial modelling is a powerful tool in the management accountant's tool bag. But as with any tool it is only as good as the person who uses it. Perhaps the greatest potential of financial models lies in the way in which they can add a variety of different ways of looking at information and its impact on strategy and future action.

To be effective in providing this additional dimension for information they have to be:

(a) built by people who understand the business;
(b) relatively simple in structure;
(c) fed with sound data; and
(d) constantly monitored and amended to reflect the real world.

The real value of a model is determined by its usefulness and not by its sophistication and elegance. The computer now allows a great deal of flexibility in the building and use of models and it should be exploited to its limit by management accountants.

12 Strategic Modelling

Information technology is in itself an important strategic consideration for most organisations. One of those strategic considerations is to what extent IT can support the strategic financial management of the organisation.

The potential for IT support in strategic decision making is considerable. In this chapter it is possible to give only a flavour of this potential.

12.1 The role of models

The basic idea of models has been discussed in Chapter 11, but it will help to re-examine some of the main points. A model is a representation of reality. Whether the model is a physical, three-dimensional model – such as an airframe for testing in a wind tunnel – or an abstract symbolic model using mathematics to define it, it is nevertheless only a model.

Financial models are a symbolic representation of a business, or part of a business. They are, by their very nature, probabilistic; they are neither true nor false in their predictions.

IT provides a mechanism for constructing financial models by using the enormous capacity that is available on computers to store and manipulate vast volumes of data very quickly. Of course, the blueprints for the construction of the models come from the understanding that people have of the business process. This understanding is converted into mathematical matrices into which data is entered and then processed according to the rules (formulae) that define data dependencies.

This chapter examines four strategic financial management models:

- the business/economic model;
- the market model;
- the investment model; and
- the cash-flow model.

These four have been chosen because most organisations will be involved in taking strategic financial decisions in all these areas.

The intention here is not to display the specific mathematics that might be involved, but to suggest ways in which IT can support the decision process. For each model 'critical impactors' can be identified. These are usually independent variables which cause significant fluctuations in strategic outcomes. It is these 'critical impactors' that have to be carefully monitored and predicted on the basis of the latest and best possible information available.

12.2 The business/economic model

No business is a closed system. There is constant interaction with the environment in which the business operates. The aim of the business/economic model is to try to represent the business as an element of that wider environment.

The first step then is to identify the *environmental variables,* which might be, for example, economic growth rates, exchange rates, interest rates, specific industry factors such as commodity price forecasts, and so on. The intention is to identify the degree to which these variables have an impact on the business. To do this the primary business model must be constructed.

The *business variables* are those which define the business, and in essence are the balance sheet elements and the operating elements (profit and loss account). If the business is a large conglomerate then it will be preferable to construct business models for each of the subsidiary businesses and to construct a consolidation model.

In the case of multinational businesses it will be necessary to identify different environmental variables for each country and apply them to the consolidated business model for each country before consolidating these outcomes into the corporate model.

The use of IT enables what is already known about the business variables through the financial accounting system to be adjusted to create the business model. Budgeting systems are perhaps the nearest thing that will exist to the business model.

Once the business/economic model is constructed – and it must be remembered that it has to be capable of rapid and continuous adaptation – it can be used to test a wide range of possible outcomes for different strategies. The beauty of the business/economic model is that it can provide a means of gaining a greater understanding of the 'impact' of the different environmental variables and it is from this that 'critical impactors" can be identified.

There is, in other words, an important learning process at work when the business/economic model is used. In fact the more often the model is used and the more experience people have in using it, the greater their understanding of environmental factors becomes. This is very important for day-to-day decision-making and for keeping in touch with the latest environmental information.

A warning note: it is easier and better to have many small integrated models than one large all-encompassing model. The reality of most large businesses is that they operate as many small units and environmental factors do not always impact on these separate parts in the same way.

In addition, with modern IT networks managers can have wide access to the business/economic model, at least to that part of it with which they are primarily concerned. They can feed in data that becomes available and quickly assess the implications for their business unit. In this way the business/economic model is a management tool and not something that the 'planning department' plays about with.

12.3 The market model

The market model is an extension, or more detailed version, of the market element of the business model. It is concerned only with those variables which affect sales revenue.

The market model can be looked at (segmented) in terms of products, customers, geography, demography, etc., and the basic variables of volume and price established in each of the segments with some indication of sensitivity each might have on outcomes. Once again the 'critical impactors' are sought. Will price fluctuations within a certain range have a critical impact or not?

Distribution variables might have a significant part to play, and in retailing factors such as shelf- and/or floor-space will be important. Other variables, such as promotional spend and brand loyalty, can be included to assess the effects of multi-variable impact. For example, will a certain increase in promotional spend plus a certain reduction in price have a significant impact on certain products in certain segments? Exercises like this using the model can provide a wonderful learning tool for management.

Monitoring actual results in the marketplace will provide information for the adaptation of the rules applying to data dependencies. But history – even the most recent – is not always a good basis for modelling. Market research can provide invaluable data for the construction and/or adaptation of the market model. What usually happens is that assumptions and beliefs gained from a historical knowledge of the market can be significantly altered by new data.

The market model can also have competition factors built in to deaden the effect of, for example, price decreases; or to assess the effect of new entrants to the market with a lower cost base and hence a lower price but a higher margin.

There are many possibilities that can be built into the market model and with the speed and power of the computer these can be manipulated at many levels. The outcome of this is a multidimensional view of the market that can be presented graphically and so provide insights for strategic thinking that might not otherwise be possible.

Of course, marketing strategy has to be a part of broader corporate strategies for production, purchasing, people, etc. Nevertheless there is considerable potential for examining the possible effects of fluctuations in the key variables so that the 'critical impactors' can be identified and focused on.

12.4 The investment model

The investment model is a well-known model often going under the nickname 'capex'. It has three prime aspects:

- asset maintenance (including replacement);
- business/market development (including acquisitions); and
- research and development.

Using IT, models can be built for each aspect, and at many levels to cover the needs of even the largest multinational. These can then be consolidated to give a

JOHN MOORES UNIVERSITY
AVRIL ROBARTS LRC
TEL. 0151 231 4022

complete view of the strategic possibilities for optimising investment opportunities within various constraints for borrowing, gearing, raising equity, etc.

The power of the computer – the sheer amount of data that can be stored and manipulated – makes investment modelling perfectly feasible.

The *asset maintenance model* will use the organisation's asset database to project replacement programmes based on a variety of different policies. These can include possibilities for early asset replacement based on new developments and for taking a life-cycle costing approach to investment decisions.

The *business/market development model* is more about the returns that can be made from different strategies and will involve variables such as different investment returns for funds, potential market optimisation opportunities, borrowing exposure, desired earnings per share, and so on.

The object is to construct a model which will provide insights on the variables which will have greatest impact on the bottom line. This is an area that is fraught with difficulties because of the unknown risk variables involved. Sometimes the strategy that is followed is based more on faith than the model's predictions. You might remember the predictions made for BSkyB in its early days, when the number of satellite dishes sold could be directly linked to forecast results. There was probably a computer-based model working away to provide this data, although whether its predictions were the basis of the strategic direction followed is another question. But there is no doubt that the management had clearly identified the 'critical impactor' and made it a focus of their strategy.

The *research and development model* is yet another difficult, yet vital, strategic investment decision area. Of course, the extent of its implications for the business's success will vary greatly, from computer software and pharmaceutical companies at one end of the scale to quarrying and retailing at the other end.

In all these areas of investment modelling evaluation techniques such as discounted cash flow, payback and others can be built in as standard features. In addition, probability analysis can be used to give 'the most likely' outcome from a wide range of possibilities.

12.5 The cash-flow model

Perhaps the cash-flow model is the best known and the most used of strategic financial models. It is concerned with the primary variables concerned with converting business activities into cash. The key variables are the inflows and outflows and the speed, or cycle, of the flows.

The cycle of the flows can be counted in days and might appear as follows:

Sales cash inflow

50%	30 days
25%	40 days
15%	55 days
5%	60 days
3%	80 days
2%	never

Using the model this can be applied to current and projected sales to produce the expected cash flow. What would the position be if the cycle variable was changed in terms of percentages and number of days? What would the impact be on sales cash inflow? Would the benefit of offering cash discounts be worthwhile?

Depending on the business the cash-inflow cycle could be a 'critical impactor' and, by focusing on this area, a significant improvement could be made in cash flow.

Other variables could be the supplier payment cycle, wages and salaries cycles (although these tend to be fixed rather than variable), 'capex' plans, and so on.

The value of the cash-flow model is in being able to test a range of possible impacts from a number of strategic decisions and then to focus where the impact appears to be greatest.

The IT model can present the range of possible outcomes in graphical form and show the typical inflow/outflow graph, and the bank position graph. These can then be varied by the various alternatives being tested on the model.

12.6 Summary

The benefits of IT via the construction of strategic financial management models are a significant contribution to strategic decision-making in five ways.

- They enable 'critical impactors' to be identified and then focused on. This is perhaps the most important aspect of modelling. It is often described as 'sensitivity analysis' because the approach tests the sensitivity of outcomes to certain variables.

- The continuing importance of the 'critical impactors' can be evaluated from current data and from updating the model. Using the BSkyB example: when the market for satellite dishes declines a more important impactor may be people not renewing contracts.

- It is possible to test ideas and assumptions about what the impact of different strategic directions might be before testing them in the real world. In this way, although risk can never be removed, some obvious high-risk decisions might be identified and the risk reduced or avoided.

- Once constructed (this can be quite a costly exercise, although with modern spreadsheets should not be a deterrent) the models can be used over and over again and continuously improved from experience and a better understanding of the business.

- Building and using financial management models as a management tool is in itself an important and valuable learning process for decision-makers.

Last but not least, an important reminder: no matter how tried and tested they are, models are exactly that – they are not the real world.

13 Product-contribution Analysis: a Computer-based Model

The theory of 'product life cycles' is now well established in marketing lore. The idea that a product has a determinable life is both interesting and has a historical validity, particularly in the field of IT hardware and software.

For many organisations the idea of 'product life cycles' may be a reality, but not necessarily apparent in the short term. Following the usual idea of the stages being birth, growth, maturity, decline, death, and using the idea of contribution generated as a measure of where the product is in its life cycle, the life cycle can be depicted as in Figure 13.1.

Figure 13.1: Product life cycle

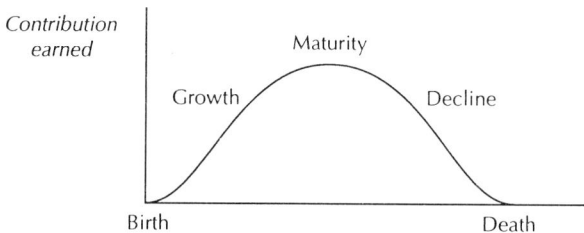

It is clear that most organisations will need a portfolio of products in different stages of their life cycles in order to maintain a progressive financial performance.

Product strategy then becomes a matter of deciding where to invest development and marketing spend to ensure a balanced portfolio and optimise the contribution from current stable of products.

To do this calls for constant monitoring of product performance and the ability to test the predicted outcomes of a variety of product strategies.

13.1 A case study – Reward Chemicals

What follows is a case study of a business that used IT to create a product-contribution model which provides continuous information on:

- product life cycles;
- product status;
- product mix.

Reward Chemicals produces three product ranges: herbicides, insecticides and fertilisers. Within each range there are a number of products. Each product had several package types/sizes. The products are produced from a range of standard chemicals which are processed through mixing, drying and packaging stages. The plant capacity is limited without considerable capital expenditure. Management wishes to optimise product mix to increase profits.

The first step in the model is to gather direct cost information from production (activity-based costing). This is used to deal with most of the production costs. Sales and marketing costs that can be identified directly to products are also included in the direct costs.

The model is then fed with the information of sales income generated per product per order, and the product contribution calculated by using the standard product direct cost. (Standard product direct costs are varied monthly, based on the management accounting information.)

Once the model has calculated the product contributions it produces:

▪ an individual product life-cycle chart;
▪ a product-contribution map;
▪ a current contribution chart; and
▪ an optimum product mix statement.

Individual product life-cycle chart

This shows for each product, separately, within its product group and within its product range the moving annual average current contribution. This measure is used to iron out (to some degree) seasonal fluctuations. The chart appears in Figure 13.2.

Figure 13.2: Individual product life-cycle chart

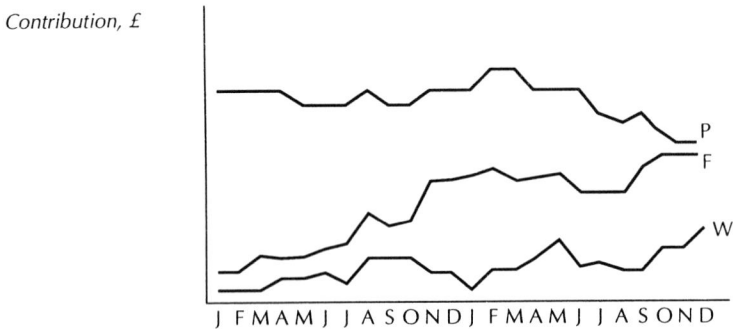

In the product life-cycle chart the three products shown are in the insecticide range:

▪ *Pestoff*, which is a mature product that might be at the start of its decline;
▪ *Flyswot*, which is a new product that is in the growth stage and has a lot of potential;
▪ *Waspkil*, which is also new and is slowly growing.

It will be important to encourage both Flyswot and Waspkil to reach maturity as Pestoff declines. Different ideas can be tested using the model to see what might happen.

Product-contribution map

Figure 13.3 shows the status of products by plotting both the sales income generated by the product and the percentage contribution generated from these sales. The map is produced on the basis of the annual moving average.

Figure 13.3: Product-contribution map

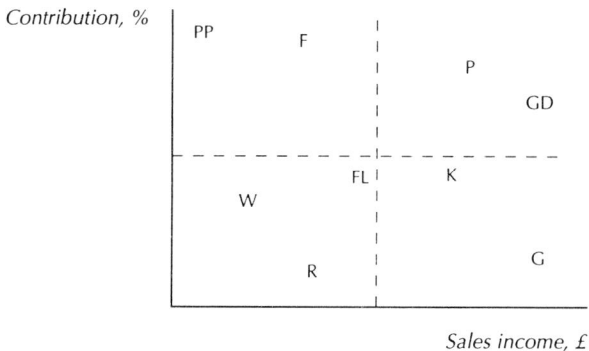

Contribution, %

Sales income, £

Figure 13.3 shows four categories or status of product:

- Dogs   Low contribution %, low sales income
- Pigs   Low contribution %, high sales income
- Stars   High contribution %, low sales income
- Cash cows   High contribution %, high sales income

The categories above are based loosely on the labels originated by the Boston Consulting Group in its product portfolio matrix, but using a contribution approach rather than the market share and penetration approach of BCG.

Using the contribution approach, the different product categories provide an indication of product potential as follows:

- *Dogs*   Little scope for development: any further spending on marketing will reduce the contribution % and attempts to increase the contribution % by price increases will probably reduce sales income.
- *Pigs*   Little scope for development except to increase prices and lose sales income. Doing this will release limited resources for other products and contribution % might increase.
- *Stars*   Here there is scope for development into cash cows because even a fall in contribution % can be accepted for increased sales income.

- *Cash cows* These are mature products producing optimum contribution and the usual strategy is to try to maintain this position for as long as possible.

The contribution map element of the system has a feature which shows the direction in which the product has moved since the last map by inserting an arrow which can be made to flash (Figure 13.4). Movements can be interpreted as:

- *North*   Increased contribution %
- *South*   Reduced contribution %
- *East*   Increased sales income
- *West*   Reduced sales income

It can be seen that:

- NE movements are beneficial;
- SW movements are not beneficial; and
- NW and SE movements may or may not be beneficial.

Of course, particular movements will depend on the product strategy being followed.

To the map can also be added a series of contribution 'equalisation curves' which show where the contribution generated, i.e. sales income × contribution % are equal. Any movement across these curves to the *east* is good, and to the *west* bad. The contribution map model can be used to test ideas for product strategy to see if products move in the desired direction.

Figure 13.4: Product-contribution map with arrows

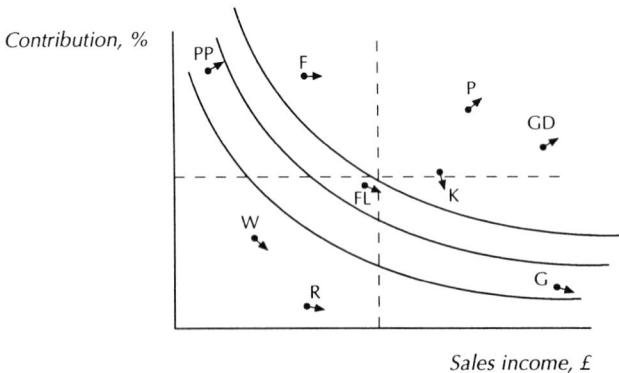

Current contribution chart

Using the system a picture of total current contribution for any combination of period or average can be produced – for example, the chart for moving annual total, or moving annual average, or this month actual, and so on. Different strategies can also be tried. Figure 13.5 shows a current contribution chart.

Figure 13.5: Current contribution chart

Rootgrow
Popup
Waspkil
Floranosh
Flyswot
Killall
Pestoff
Grassguard

The product contribution chart can be built up on screen product by product and the actual value of contribution displayed. The importance of products in the total picture can then be compared with their status on the map.

Optimum product mix statement

The optimum product mix in Reward Chemicals depends on the company's limited capacity, so part of the system calculates the current product contribution per factor of limiting capacity. This is then used to produce a statement of the volumes of all products in the total product range that need to be produced and sold to optimise contribution.

This statement can then be used in conjunction with the other information in the system to test and arrive at what seems to be the most appropriate product strategy.

Using the system

When the system was first used in its fully operating version a major product strategy change was decided on. This involved taking Greenery, a 'pig' which used a large proportion of capacity for a very small contribution, and redeveloping it as a new product. The new product, Greenery Plus, was sold in smaller quantities at a higher price because it was twice as good. Greenery was still available but only in large sizes and the price was increased. Within 18 months Greenery Plus was a high-selling cash cow and Greenery had disappeared.

Through this single strategy existing capacity was able to generate quadrupled profits. Since then the product range has been simplified particularly in respect to packaging options.

13.2 Summary

The approach described here would not have been possible without IT. Of course, the theories involved stand alone from the IT, but it is the application of IT that makes it possible to convert the theories into a practical day-to-day management tool.

14 Executive Information Systems

The following words are an extract from an article written by an EIS salesman. They suggest a panacea that is still far from the reach of most managers.

> EIS is the key which unlocks the power and value of computer investment by giving managers access to corporate data, on screen, in an attractive and intuitive manner, allowing them to make better, more informed and timely decisions.

Many holes could be picked in this statement but one will suffice: the idea that computer-generated information can be intuitive is ridiculous. Intuition is non-rational knowledge. The computer can only be rational.

Modern computer workstations offer managers a wide range of facilities that can enable them to produce really effective personal information systems. But few managers have the skills to make use of these facilities, and for those that do it is difficult to get at the data that they need to make decisions. The aim of EIS is to make it possible to bring together data and facilities to present information in an attractive and usable way. To do this they offer a range of tools including:

- a simple system for accessing data;
- a database;
- a means of manipulating data; and
- a means of producing a report and/or a screen display.

14.1 A system for accessing data

This provides a series of menu selections which, when chosen, instigate search and retrieve routines, which may include a network link to some other database. The data required is found and brought back to the workstation where it is loaded into the EIS database. From here it can be manipulated and/or displayed. The EIS provides the tool for doing this work, but the data to be retrieved and its source have to be input by managers when they set up their EIS.

As a means of getting and presenting information the EIS is a very useful device. Without it busy managers face the task of logging on to the system they want to access and then retrieving the data they want. They may then need to access another system for more data, and so on. This can be a tedious and frustrating process. The EIS overcomes these frustrations.

However, for the EIS to be effective managers have to know the data they need and where it can be found. In addition it has to be held in a form that can be accessed by the EIS and structured so that it can go into the EIS's own database. This is a much bigger problem than might be at first imagined.

To obtain data from different systems so that it is structured to fit into a predefined database format means that each of the systems to be accessed must be using the same data-formatting protocols and the same database management system. This is often not the case, and even when it is the retrieval routines have to be programmed to pick up the data in a specific way. What this all means is that EIS works best when all other systems are defined from the beginning with the EIS in mind.

14.2 The EIS database

This provides a means for locally storing data that can be accessed by other EIS tools. It becomes the personal database of the manager and contains the information thought to be pertinent to the decision-making of the manager concerned.

It can hold data in the form in which it is retrieved and then also hold data after the manipulation carried out by the manager. For example, data could be collected on product costs and product sales from different systems. These could then be brought together to produce product contribution and this result stored in the EIS database.

In this way managers can construct and keep available information that they find particularly useful and as their needs change so they can change the nature of the information they gather into their EIS.

14.3 Manipulating data

In the EIS this means using the data that has been gathered and by sorting it, merging it, running calculations, etc. producing additional information more relevant to managers' needs. The manipulation processes can be likened to spreadsheets; in fact in some EISs that is exactly what they are.

14.4 Reporting and displaying information in the EIS

This is done via some form of report generator linked to a graphical user interface (GUI). The system usually works by taking data from the database and presenting it in the format defined by the manager. This means that managers have to take the time and trouble to learn and understand the reporting aspect of the EIS if they want to present information in an interesting way.

14.5 The potential of EIS

So where are we today with EIS potential?

- Excellent computer facilities exist for accessing, manipulating and presenting information.
- Managers are increasingly computer literate and able to understand and use modern software products.
- Management accountants have a better understanding of data flows and decision information analysis.
- Business activities are getting faster and worldwide communication is instantaneous.

The real-world EIS is a complex, multilevelled one, with both formal and informal information inputs. It also includes all the manager's experience, training and personal knowledge. To suggest that this can all be placed onto a computer system is, to say the least, ill-informed. There is also a great deal of information which managers do not seek and which arrives uninvited. Much of this information is picked up 'in passing' or received via the 'grapevine'. And anyone who derides or degrades these sources of information does not understand the nature of human communication.

A real EIS would be a system where managers enter the decisions they have to take. The system, which has been previously programmed to provide information specified as relevant for each decision, then provides a schedule of that information in a format ready for use. This 'formal' information can be added to all the other information to hand and the decision taken. The system should also allow managers to record the information that might have been useful but which was not available.

In this way – and with constant interaction between the manager and the system – a personalised information system could be built up and constantly honed until it was really able to serve the manager. It is imperative that we look at information and its use in a personalised way. We are all different. We have different approaches to decision-making and need different information even for the same decisions.

Some of the information needed will be common to the decision, no matter who takes it, but this is usually the numerical data which is often the least important element.

The speed of business activities is much faster than it used to be in marketing, production, distribution and administration. The instantaneous nature of global communications is forcing a rethink as to how information is processed and managed.

In line with the speed at which things are happening managers have to rethink what is meant by decision-making. It does not mean taking command; it does not mean telling people what to do; it does not mean taking action. Decision-making means making informed choices. This means that examining the range and scope of options available is the most critical aspect of decision-making – and it is in this area that managers limit themselves to the options of experience and practice.

No EIS will help managers to seek creative and innovative options. And in a sense a system which feeds predefined information to established decision areas may further limit the search for new options.

Decision-making problems apart, executive information systems are certainly a part of the answer to harmonising the use of interlinked databases and communication channels, but we should not get carried away with their potential. They do little to improve security and control of information, and they also do little to improve the quality of information available for decision-making. The provision of touch-sensitive screens and the use of mice and icons are little more than gimmicks – even if they are useful.

14.6 The management consultant's role

Perhaps this is where the management accountant fits into the picture. The greater the understanding of data flows and decision information analysis, the more likely it is that the information managers want will be available. Management accountants are the primary source of formal information for decision-making, and it is perhaps they who need to move away from rigid regular (monthly) reporting to the more exciting and useful areas of continuous information processing and EIS.

The management accountant's role in future will involve the creation of truly effective EIS and personalised information systems for managers. This role involves three things:

- helping managers to analyse their decision-making information needs;
- building the appropriate EIS structures and models;
- ensuring the availability of the primary data.

Defining managers' information needs is perhaps one of the most difficult of these three tasks. This is partly because managers are themselves unsure about what they need, and partly because management accountants find it hard to see things from the manager's viewpoint. The only approach is for management accountants and managers to sit down together and to look at the decisions managers take and the information they use to do this. If this task is tackled over a period of time then both management accountants and managers will gain a growing understanding of their needs.

Building the appropriate EIS means acquiring the most appropriate software and learning to use it so that it can handle the needs of managers in the best way. Management accountants can work closely with managers to build the data-access routines, construct the data-manipulation models, and format the reports.

Making sure the primary data exists is the other important part of the job. This is where management accountants should be able to use their knowledge of the business transactions and their data-management skills to the full. Data collection, verification and validation is an essential part of basic information systems design and management. If it isn't done effectively than even the best EIS will serve only to misinform and mislead.

14.7 Decision support

This approach to ensuring managers get the information they need is increasingly being referred to as decision support. This does not necessarily mean only computer-based decision support, but also the decision support that comes from being able to communicate effectively with managers and to discuss their needs so that both management accountants and managers learn about what information can be made available and the technology resources available to do it.

EIS is part of decision support. It can be an important part, but it will not provide answers to decision problems. EIS will only be effective in an environment where decision-making is fully understood and where the role of information in the decision-making process is clear and well defined. So EIS will enhance those situations where decision support is already operating well. Where decision support is inadequate EIS may well serve to make it even worse.

The journey towards personalised information systems is not easy. The resources exist, but the road is unclear. It is like having the finest four-wheel-drive vehicle full of the best equipment and stores and sitting on the edge of a desert without a map, a compass or a watch. Even the best driver would find that hard going, and would make many wrong turns.

What managers want is the information they need, when they need it, in the form they need it. It makes no difference whether this is from a computer screen, a printed report, or a voice over the telephone, as long as it can be trusted and acted on with confidence.

If EIS meets this requirement then fine; otherwise it is just another way to sell hardware and software.

14.8 Summary

An EIS is a combination of several software tools that enable managers to retrieve and manipulate information. With the use of networks growing and the increased power of PCs it is perfectly feasible for informed managers to create the situation where they have the information they need, quite literally, at the touch of a button.

Index

technofear 30, 101

technology
  see also computer systems
  CSF 99–100
  future possibilities 9–10
  people 29–32

textual presentations 118–21

theory, information 61–79

trading partners, external data sources
  109

transactional data 49
  processing 19

trends 6, 21
  automated administration 20

truth traps, presentation pitfalls 129

uncertainty, decision-making 109–10

understanding 56

usefulness assessments, relevance
  reporting 117

user support, computer systems 28

value 55, 67, 89–95
  information overload 81

value-added networks (VANs) 7

VANs *see* value-added networks

variables
  business/economics models 138
  cash-flow models 140–1
  financial models 134
  investment models 140
  market models 139
  sensitivity analysis 135

videos, presentation 126

views, relational databases 78–9

viruses, Internet 41

visual communications 40

voice systems
  computer systems 127
  future possibilities 10

warehousing, data 81–4

web browsers 36

what-if analysis 110
  financial models 135

windows, HCI 28–9

windows of opportunity, decision-making
  70–3

word processing 26

work 23–34
  design area 24
  HCI 27–9
  history 4
  information handling 25
  mechanisation/automation 23–4
  methods 25–6
  service industries 25
  trends 5

World Wide Web (WWW) 35–6

WWW *see* World Wide Web

younger people, computer literacy 3–4